Praise for the travel writing of Sybille Bedford

"Sybille Bedford is such a good writer . . . and her travel pieces contain her most beautiful writing. She has an idiosyncratic style, allusive and personal, like carefully stylized chat. She is a master of the adjective and the comma, of the long, supple, thrilling list that unfolds before one like one of the scenes she describes. Her descriptions are exact—the interior of a hotel is like 'a polished walnut.' She is funny—on foreigners' English, *de rigueur* but irresistible (the Italian restaurant where you can eat 'foot & bean' and 'humids,' the Yugoslav bookstore where you can read Džek London, Mark Tven, and Džejn Ostin). She is sharp and unillusioned—on Italian noise ('either you are Italian or Italian-built and don't hear it, or you aren't and you do and it is unbearable') and on Yugoslav crowds ('their overall aspect is one of sallowness, burdens and poor clothes'). But she is positive; she finds something to love or admire everywhere."

—Carole Angier, *New Statesman*

"Even palate-philistines, who merely eat to live, will be deeply moved by Sybille Bedford's meals and wines recollected in tranquillity. . . . Mrs. Bedford provocatively defines travel as 'an engagement of the ego *v.* the world.' Then, in superb sketches of Denmark, Portugal, Venice, Switzerland, and Yugoslavia, she cuts the ground from under her own definition: no egocentric writer could so deftly distil, in a few thousand words, 'the spirit of place.' . . . Outstanding."

—Dervla Murphy, *The Times Literary Supplement*

"Who does this remind you of: 'Beware of large round loaves that look like dark country bread: that is *brua,* maize bread, and as heavy as wet cement'? Bedford's writing on food can be compared to Elizabeth David's. Of the same generation, of a similarly cosmopolitan background, they share a tone of voice that is lucid and authoritative, just a little bossy. Such a marvellous acerbity, based as it has been on a lifetime of experience, of absolute confidence in what is what, has more or less died out in the newer generation of ignoramus food writers. . . . Her *joie de vivre,* her sensitivity makes her our prize chronicler of sensuous experience."

—Fiona McCarthy, *The Times*

Books by Sybille Bedford

A Visit to Don Otavio
A Traveller's Tale from Mexico

A Legacy
A Novel

The Best We Can Do
The Trial of Dr. Adams

The Faces of Justice
A Traveller's Report

A Favourite of the Gods
A Novel

A Compass Error
A Novel

Aldous Huxley
A Biography

Jigsaw: An Unsentimental Education
A Biographical Novel

As It Was
Pleasures, Landscapes and Justice

Pleasures and Landscapes
A Traveller's Tales from Europe

PLEASURES

and

LANDSCAPES

A Traveller's Tales from Europe

SYBILLE BEDFORD

Introduction by
JAN MORRIS

COUNTERPOINT

NEW YORK

The eight essays collected here first appeared in British and American periodicals
between 1954 and 2001. Six were collected by the author in her book *As It Was*,
published in Great Britain in 1990 but not published in the United States.
"A Homecoming" and "La Vie de Château" appear here in book form
for the first time.

Two poems by Arthur Rimbaud appear in the text complete and in the original
French. The epigraph is "Au Cabaret-Vert, cinq heures du soir" (October 1870).
The poem on pages 69 and 70 is "Sensation" (March 1870). The texts are those
prepared by Wyatt Mason for his bilingual edition of Rimbaud's works,
Rimbaud Complete, published by The Modern Library in 2002.

First Edition

Library of Congress Cataloging-in-Publication Data
Bedford, Sybille, 1911–
    Pleasures and landscapes : a traveller's tales from Europe / Sybille
Bedford ; introduction by Jan Morris.
        p. cm.
    Includes bibliographical references.
    ISBN 1-58243-170-1 (pbk.)
    1. Bedford, Sybille, 1911–Journeys—Europe. 2. Europe—Description
and travel. 3. Europe—Intellectual life—20th century. I. Title.

D922 .B416 2003
940.55—dc21

                                                            2002153453

Designed by Jeff Williams
Set in 11.5-point Galliard by the Perseus Books Group

Printed in the United States of America on acid-free paper that meets the
American National Standards Institute Z39-48 Standard.

Counterpoint
387 Park Avenue South
New York, N.Y. 10016

Counterpoint is a member of the Perseus Books Group.

03 04 05 / 10 9 8 7 6 5 4 3 2 1

To

LESLEY

from her nervous passenger

CONTENTS

———

Depuis huit jours, j'avais déchiré mes bottines
Aux cailloux des chemins. J'entrais à Charleroi.
— *Au Cabaret-Vert*: je demandai des tartines
De beurre et du jambon qui fût à moitié froid.

Bienheureux, j'allongeai les jambes sous la table
Verte: je contemplai les sujets très naïfs
De la tapisserie. — Et ce fut adorable,
Quand la fille aux tétons énormes, aux yeux vifs

— Celle-là, ce n'est pas un baiser qui l'épeure!
— Rieuse, m'apporta des tartines de beurre,
Du jambon tiède, dans un plat colorié,

Du jambon rose et blanc parfumé d'une gousse
*D'ail, — et m'emplit la chope immense, avec
   sa mousse*
Que dorait un rayon de soleil arriéré.

—ARTHUR RIMBAUD

———

INTRODUCTION

IT IS ONLY HUMAN that those of us who live by the
sweat of our inky fingers so often feel the urge to snatch
our fugitive essays from oblivion and confine them once
and for all within the covers of a book. For some of us, of
course, it is just a form of vanity publishing: these compi-
lations seldom make money for anyone and are fearfully
vulnerable to the critical sneer, but they stand gratifyingly
on our bookshelves, and they may give a bit of fun to our
great-grandchildren.

For others, however, it is an assertion of art's unity.
Bruce Chatwin evidently thought that the pieces collected in his *What Am I Doing Here* were an essential part
of his oeuvre. V. S. Pritchett's miscellany *At Home and
Abroad* was as worthy of his reputation as were his full-
length travel books. And this collection by Sybille
Bedford certainly clarifies her distinguished but somewhat imprecise status in the republic of letters. Everyone
knows her name, but relatively few readers, especially perhaps in America, realize the range of her gifts—novelist,
biographer, analyst of the law, travel writer, celebrant of
food, and mistress of an altogether inimitable prose.

Pleasures and Landscapes will make things clearer. It is an ideal primer. It consists of eight essays of varying length written between 1954 and 2001 for publications English and American, *Encounter* to *Esquire*. Their matter ranges from the sensations of hill walking to the best way of pronouncing Portuguese ("lop off the final vowel and as many others as laziness suggests . . ."), but their manner is one throughout: it is a deliberately but idiosyncratically literary manner. Although I suppose Mrs. Bedford was usually writing in the first place to earn a dollar or two, she never relaxes her hold upon her technique, or her determination to translate scenes and events into a kind of apotheosized reportage.

This is wonderfully exhilarating, especially since none of the essays have been touched up in retrospect, except for an occasional footnote. These really are pleasures and landscapes, as they were at the time. Norman Douglas calls Martha Gellhorn "a poppet" in the Capri of 1948. Mateus rosé is a wine to take note of in 1958. Going to Yugoslavia in the 1960s is a matter of "curiosity, tinged with apprehension." The first impact of Switzerland after World War II comes rushing back in a torrent of immaculate, efficient, complacent, polite, and prosperous images. We feel that we are not looking back at life thirty, forty, fifty years ago but *experiencing* it for ourselves, with all its joys, hazards, and surprises.

All this means that the book is entirely personal and particular. There are very few generalizations. It is all instant response and instant emotion, and Mrs. Bedford's

Introduction

unique style, though for all I know it is honed through long midnight hours, reads as though it streams out of her sensibility without preoccupation and without review. Occasionally I find it a little *too* irrepressible, especially when it comes to food (she is very interested in eating and drinking)—her "sea bream, charred and nutty," "limpid" olive oil, and fish soup of "coruscating" color may drive readers of less urbane gourmandism, like me, all the more readily to the deep-freeze Ocean Pie.

On the whole, though, the impetuous integrity is fascinating to observe. Mrs. Bedford has been writing her brilliantly individual (not to say eccentric) essays for decades, and to this day they make the work of most practitioners tame and conventional by comparison. Her piece "The Quality of Travel" is as fresh now, and as full of relevant advice, as it was when she wrote it in 1961. She says in a footnote to this book that "it is for the reader to decide what is essentially unchanged and what is changed," but I think the caveat is unnecessary. What is essential is the truth of her writing. It comes straight from the heart—the source, to my mind, not only of the best art but the best reporting too.

—*Jan Morris*

A HOMECOMING

Capri 1948

⌒THE NAPLES BOAT was on time. The crossing—
it was May—had not been too gruelling. Lightly one
stepped ashore and into the funicular, and, after a brief,
slow ascent, emerged into Piazza still warm under a late
afternoon sun.

I was elated. To be back, to be back anywhere in those
days—the year was 1948—felt a miracle. One responded
with a delirious sense of freedom, rediscovery, renewal:
the Europe for so long known to be held down in agony
and chaos, so long believed lost to us, possibly forever,
was beginning to be regained. I had spent—immense
privilege—the winter in Italy, Venice first, then Florence,
and was now living, somewhat precariously, in a back-
street hotel in Rome. I had stayed up late the night
before—all hours were precious—then left at dawn, driving south chanting poetry to myself in the car I had been
entrusted to deliver. By full morning, when the near-
empty road (not much legitimate petrol around then)

glared before me, I had to fight drowsiness till at one point there was a great jolt and I came to with the front wheel already off the road and was just able to wrench the car back on course. Jolted hard myself, I stopped—I had missed the ditch, a milestone, a tree. Out of nowhere women arose from a field crying, "Mamma mia." I braced myself to inspect the damage, but no—no dent, no buckled mudguard, no burst tire; the poor old Morris looked unscathed. I was not quite so sure about the steering as I drove on, slowly now, with circumspection, and contrite, appalled by my irresponsibility. *This was not my car.* Another hundred and forty kilometers to go, out of some two hundred and fifty. The prospect seemed long. . . . The dawn jaunt had turned into a slow, hot, anxious drive.

In the end I got there. I left the car as arranged, in a garage considered—as far as is possible in Naples—one of the less blatantly dishonest ones, and instructed them to check and, if necessary, repair the steering (the bill to go to me). After that, lunching with a friend, the young British Vice Consul, I got my second wind. Constantine FitzGibbon was with us, and Theodora—we were all high with the same postwar joy of being where we were, and I only just caught the boat to Capri.

On boarding, Constantine left me with a pill he said he'd got off a German officer he'd taken prisoner during the Italian campaign. It was a largeish capsule, a bit tacky by now, issued reputedly to keep a man efficient and alert for forty-eight hours or more without sleep. Constantine seemed to think I might need it before the day was out (I had told him whom I'd have to face). Recklessness had returned: I accepted the pill, wrapped it in a scrap of tissue, and put it in my pocket.

And now there was Capri. The island looked itself. One point about the war was that where it had not destroyed, it had conserved. Craters and ruins, yes, but no new excrescences (yet): for five and a half years the developers had been kept at bay. And in Piazza there was the usual crowd, native and tourist, assembled to wait and watch the boat arrive and passengers appear. To my surprise and pleasure I saw Martha Gellhorn. I had not expected her to meet me, but she had.

"I say," she said, "this is a glorious place." She had taken a room for me at the pensione where she was staying, a hundred feet up from Piazza. Clean and cheap. "That," I said, "would be delightful." But before we took one step further I had to tell her something. (Straight candor—with Martha anything else was unthinkable.) "I have done something very bad," I said. Then told her what had happened.

She and I had met only just over a week before at the studio flat of a man who to her was a fellow journalist and an ex-combatant (he had been parachuted into German-held Italy after Anzio and spent some intensely perilous months underground before the liberation of Rome) and to me a connection, a cousin in fact, of my stepfather, and a childhood chum. Meeting Martha Gellhorn, being addressed, being taken notice of by her, was like being exposed to a fifteen-hundred-watt chandelier: she radiated vitality, certainty, total courage. Add to this the voltage of her talk—galloping, relentlessly slangy, wry, dry, self-deprecatory, often funny. Add to this her *looks*. The honey-colored hair, shoulder-length, the intense large blue eyes, the fine-cut features, the bronzed skin, the graceful, stalwart stance. I saw her as the (very feminine) image of the Pierro delle Francesca Archangel in the National Gallery, the presented sword, the heroic yet angelic look, the slender foot poised on the dragon's head: a shining defender of the just, the oppressed, the poor.

Add her reputation. The intrepid American frontline war reporter for whom war had been the daily element when most of us had still tried to carry on with our private lives. Now she was back in Europe, in Rome at the moment, doing research on a piece, I forget about what, and she seemed to think I might be of some use. We had dinner together that night and lunch or dinner together again the next day and the next. I made no bones about the pleasure I took in her company, and a brand-new friendship began quickly. Before the week was out, Martha said that Rome had had it. (I was yet to learn about those barbarous spurts of restlessness.) I tried to point out the things she hadn't seen, had not begun to see—it was her first time in Rome (to which I was passionately attached). To no avail. She decided to look at Capri. Off tomorrow. There was a snag, though—that stinker hadn't yet come with her car.

Hiring a car in Italy was difficult or impossible, exorbitant at any rate (the Topolino had just appeared; blissfully, city streets were still crowded mainly with Vespas and pedestrians). Martha bethought herself of the Morris she had kept in storage in England during the war years and arranged for a young man, a colleague of sorts who wanted to get out to Italy, to drive it over for her. She was sure that the stinker would profiteer by giving lifts to girl-friends and cheating her over the petrol she was paying for. His name was mud already because he hadn't arrived. The situation was resolved by my offering to drive the car down to Naples for her as soon as it turned up. (I jumped at the idea of revisiting Capri, where I had old friends such as Kenneth Macpherson, who was settling there in order to look after Norman Douglas in his old age.) Martha concurred, trusted me implicitly, and went ahead by train.

Now, what had impressed me most in Martha was the absolutism of her moral standards. Looking down on much I had thought permissible in days before, I resolved to become 100 percent brave and truthful and reliable myself. This is a phenomenon well known to those who recall their first exposure to Martha Gellhorn. And now what had I done? Put myself in charge of her car after inadequate sleep. (In sober fact, I had not slept at all.)

"I did worse than your stinker," I said as we stood rooted to the spot in mid-Piazza. "I may have wrecked your car." Then I told her what had happened.

Martha looked at me with almost benign amazement. "*My,*" she said, "you might have killed yourself."

That too had occurred to me—those seconds it took to get the car in control again had been drastically lucid.

"I wouldn't have to face *you* now," I said. Martha laughed, brushing the incident aside with casual, sunny forgiveness. (Since, I have been much censured, deeply disapproved of, about many things; the Morris on the brink was never held against me.)

"Let's get into that bar and have some martinis," Martha said. We did. Presently she and I went to have dinner. (A boy porter in Piazza had taken my bag straight to the pensione.) We went to the Savoia, the small trattoria a few steps from Piazza where Norman Douglas, walking down from the Villa Truto, ate at night. One went there—the food was seldom very good, and the wine, for anyone less hardened than Norman, just not undrinkable—in the hope of his company; his privacy, though, was inviolate. The convention was to wave to him as one came in; he would call out a greeting or a warning— "Don't touch their squid tonight, my dear," or "The veal's tolerable." You might approach his table and say a few words in return. Sometimes he ate alone, usually he assembled two or three or more companions; yet, great friend or distant, one would never sit down with him unless expressly asked to do so.

That evening he had a look at Martha and liked what he saw. He called to me to bring her over. The dinner went well, it seemed to me, because of Martha and Norman's misapprehension of each other's natures. He called her "my poppet," declined to be aware that she was a formidable—and formidably committed—woman; what he chose to take in were her looks and charm. She might have been inclined to remain censorious and unamused (she had not read *Siren Land*, she had not read *South Wind;* she *had* heard of the pederasty, of which she disapproved with all the strength of her fundamentalist American Puritanism); what she took in was an exquisitely mannered old gentleman and his charm. The talk, as I remember, was chiefly about fish. Anything about the late war, Nazis, collaborators and their tortuous allegiances, would have glanced off Norman's Rabelaisian urbanity. It would not have been appropriate, and it was not attempted.

The Trattoria Savoia closed down (not early). After cheerful good-nights in Piazza—"Bless you, my poppets"—Norman stumped off for his steep walk home with pocket torch and stick. Martha and I went to our pensione, where a key had been left for us to find. The rooms, even under the weak bulb light, showed up clean and white, but they were stuffy, the shutters being closed. Owing to the peculiar topography of Capri back streets, the windows were near ceiling high: to get to them and undo those shutters one had to climb onto a pair of wooden stools. This we did and reached the small squares of open window—and there were Mauresque rooftops, stars, night air.

"Isn't this delectable?" Martha said. It was. Jasmine, citrus, oleander, warm stone, a hint of sea . . . We drew it in, leaning into the night, our elbows on the windowsill, our toes on the wobbly stools.

"We must stay up here," Martha said. "We don't have to go to bed yet in those stuffy rooms. Let's stay up here by the window. Let's watch the dawn come up. I want to talk." We did talk. Martha talked. I can still feel us as we stood balanced on those stools, heads out in the air, like two characters in a surrealist stage production. Martha talked about Ernest, about Spain, about the angle of the Nationalists' fire on the Hotel Astoria in Madrid, the safer exposure of some rooms at the Dorchester in the London Blitz. Ernest, she said, had taught her about ballistics. She talked of her own ride (unauthorized) on the naked floor of an Air Force bomber, of the ascent towards Cassino, of living with Ernest, being married to Ernest. He did not come out well. There are always two sides to anything going on between two people, but this did not come home to me during that night's talk. It was riveting, as Martha would say: I felt privileged—*I was captivated.* We were still standing, straining towards the air: there was no sign of dawn yet in the sky.

At one point I had felt in my pocket for the capsule in the crumpled bit of tissue, the German officer's pill. And I took it.

THE QUALITY
OF TRAVEL

France and Italy 1961

⌐⤙ A PART, A LARGE PART, of travelling is an engagement of the ego *v.* the world. The world is transport, the roads, the clerks behind the counters who deal out tickets, mail, messy money, keys; it is the porters, the waiters, the tourist industry, the natives, the weather. The world is hydra-headed, as old as the rocks and as changing as the sea, enmeshed inextricably in its ways. The ego wants to arrive at places safely and on time. It wants to be provided with entertainment, color, quiet, strong coffee, strong drink, matches it can strike, and change for a large paper note. It wants to find a room ready, warmth, cool, hangers, the right voltage, an ashtray, and enough clean towels. It wants the shops to be open and dinner at six-thirty or at half past ten P.M. It wants to be soothed, reassured, attended to, left in peace. It doesn't want to be stared at. It wants to be made to feel competent, generous, knowledgeable, and of accepted looks. It wants to find everything just as it expected, only rather better. It also wants to find the unexpected, but it wants that to be manageable. And whatever it wants, it wants it *now*.

It is not a pretty state, but it is one that is not easy to resist. Foreign travel is a precipitant: as home and office and familiar responsibilities recede, the man outside the ego, unless he is a gypsy, of saintly detachment, or a travelling statesman, becomes the baby or the monkey in the pram; he *is* a bundle of wants at the mercy of his environment. To himself he is alone. To the world he is myriad. For every traveller who goes disgruntled, there will be tomorrow's carload, busload, trainload. If *he* does not come back, someone awfully like him will. The traveller is expendable.

The dice have always been loaded. In most centuries travel was simply frightful. The first movements of mankind across the surface of the earth were blind massed wanderings, beset with dim perils, liable to end in extinction. Nobody in those times stirred alone. Later on, displacement became more conscious and more organized: navigation, messengers from Rome, legions on the march. The professionals moved, the seasoned, the dedicated, the passionately curious, the greedy. As travel became more individual, it became more heroic, the aims more high-flown—India, the Tomb of Christ, the Boundaries of the Universe, Gold. . . . The hardships, the uncertainty, the odds against arrival were staggering. In ship, on horse, in armor, trudging beside the donkey and the sack of Bibles, racked on wheels, the knight, the pilgrim, the conquistador, the itinerant quack, the trader swaying with the caravan, the Jesuit embarked for China, the slave in the hold, the showman to the fairground, the bold, the privileged, the meek, all stood to brave the portent of the sudden cloud, the speck on the ocean, the swirl of wind in the sand, the threat at the crossroads. All were prey to filth, disease, rapacity, and the routine ferocity of man to man. Those who were not garroted for their purse were likely to be knifed by a fanatic. Those who were fleeced at the inn might find themselves sold into captivity as well. No one was sure to wake to a new day.

By the eighteenth century rigors and perils had hardly abated. Voltaire's *Candide,* though a professed work of fiction, is a realistic travelogue of the time. So were, in due course, *Childe Harold* and *Don Juan.* Yet the scope of travel, if not its mechanics, was softening, was getting humanized, as it were. Men travelled to enlarge their education, to look at the world not to seize it; they travelled to seek health and took their families; to buy and carry home works of art—they were travelling at last for pleasure. Poets were crossing the Alps, Milord was in his carriage with his valet and the bulldog and the brace of marmosets under the coachman's seat: the era of the amateur traveller, the traveller for travel's sake, was on its way.

Gradually, very gradually, at least within a tamed circle of Western Europe, the starker dangers diminished. The discomforts remained. Mud, snow, dust, the rutted road, the bolting horses, the axle giving way; dirt, exorbitance, the doubtful bed; the delays, the waiting, the *distance.* It took eighteen days from Paris to Rome—if you were in a hurry, that was, and under favorable conditions. The Napoleonic wars did not help, yet they did not hinder. Curious as it may seem to us, war in the past was never an entire obstacle to private travel. Then steam came, and all was changed. For the first time in the lives of men and beasts, locomotion, the assisted way of getting from place to place, was quick, almost safe, and cheap; no sooner was it quick and cheap than it became luxurious. When it was technically possible to satisfy it, there was a large—though by contemporary standards limited—and discriminating demand. The nineteenth-century well-to-do lived well at home; they were not going to live less well now wherever they were or went on land or sea. Ingenious commercialism and the opulent new appetites built the transatlantic liners, the Grand Babylon hotels, railway sleeping cars, Monte Carlo, Torquay, Saratoga Springs. Plush, mahogany, and conspicuous space in public places, pilastered halls, the champagne bucket, roasts cradled in silver trolleys wheeled along the well-set tables d'hôte, the subdued, well-trained servants in place of the hordes of ruffianly soup-stained waiters—such were the complements of the steam engine and industrial change, the props of the brief gilded age of travel that flourished until 1914.

Would *we* have enjoyed it? First of all, would many of us have been *able* to enjoy it? It seems to be axiomatic now that the pleasures of good living then were only for the substantial rich. Yet I think that dollar for dollar, pound for golden sovereign, the answer to the second question is, yes. The many of us who today are able to travel at all would also have been able to afford a helping from the Edwardian fleshpots. It is tricky to determine what anything really cost at any given time. Did the bottle of five-star brandy at five shillings take longer or less time to earn than the bottle at £3/10/0 in 1961? But it would not be wrong to assume that, highball for imperial pint of Veuve Clicquot, ocean passages, hotel rooms, restaurant meals, and drink took if anything a rather smaller slice out of a person's yearly income than it would today. But then the full price of any commodity cannot be reckoned solely by the cash that comes out of the consumer's pocket. Smooth travel was possible largely because many people contributed their services to it for small pay. The great chefs of the age, in London, on the Riviera, in Switzerland (if we are to believe Arnold Bennett, who went thoroughly into such matters, and my own father, who frequented cooks and sat in kitchens in the way other gentlemen of his time frequented jockeys and the paddock), commanded the kind of salaries we associate with bullfighters and opera stars. Headwaiters and hall porters retired to sunny villas on their amassed tips. But the many, who polished the boots, carried the trunks, and wiped the plates of the relatively few, worked, according to the economic structure then prevailing, long hours and for wages that were—relatively *and* absolutely—low.

The other big reason for the traveller's steady comfort was of course that the supply still exceeded the demand. There were fewer people on the planet, and fewer of them, for good cause or bad, moved about. Hotels, restaurants, and liners were seldom full up. The traveller was the customer, and the customer ruled the roost.

"Kitchen's shut," "I'm afraid we can't, sir," "*Monsieur, c'est trop tard,*" "*Chiuso!*" were words he never heard. Instead, *he* said "My consommé is weak." (See the travel manuals.) "This truffle has not a good color. The sauce is too thin. There is shot in these quail. The cream in this pudding has not set. The claret is too warm/too cold/is corked. Take it away." "Very good, sir." And the somme-lier at the Majestic knew, and the manager knew, and the shareholders knew, that if another bottle of Pichon-Longueville '04 was not swiftly forthcoming, the chances were that this guest would be dining at the Hôtel Splendide tomorrow night.

Well then, *would* we have enjoyed it? Now, being what we are, and used to what we're getting now, very much indeed in some respects and rather less in others. There would have been less occasion for frustration, dis-appointment, anxiety. Take departure. It would *not* have been a long, traffic-bound drive to the airport or to the railway station. There would have been no herding, chan-nelling, queuing, standing, waiting, hanging about. The trains at least *left* on time. At 11:04 your ordeal, if you hap-pened to suffer from travel fever, was over. (Sooner, if you had chosen to occupy your place half an hour before.) There you were, with your luggage stacked above your head and nothing more to worry about than your neigh-bor's cigar. You didn't have to live through the takeoff; you didn't have to think about the landing. Wind and weather, except in the extremes of blizzard, were none of your concern. You could open your magazine, book a seat in the dining car, unstop a flask: you could, in today's so cherished word, relax.

The hotels (where there were hotels) were well built, the bedrooms were larger, the wardrobes deeper, a door shut stayed shut. The Victorian plumbing across the corridor was first rate, but in the room itself there was likely to be a stand with a pitcher and basin, slop pail, and carafe. Horror of present horrors: no running water.

As for the food. Was it really so very good? What did it taste like? Like lobster? Or like a sauce glued to some substance? I do not know because, like most of us, I never ate it. Like the voice of Adelina Patti, Edwardian dinner parties are now the stuff of legend. Not entirely yet, as there are survivors and we have the menus and the cookery books. The recipes are, as we know, elaborate. (They are also of a high technical excellence of their kind, the product of a prodigious amount of hard work, thought, and skill, and the material called for was the best there is: *fresh* butter, *fresh* vegetables, new-laid eggs, home-raised meat. Only the game was high.) The elaboration itself was a natural enough development; there is always a point where prosperity touches again on barbarism, where sober opulence turns to variations for variations' sake, to refinement, to over-refinement, to vulgarity. After Greece, Rome (and the Roman banquet). After the massive façade, baroque; after baroque, papier mâché. On the gastrological level, a society had been eating solid food through the bulk of a century; now it wanted to ring some changes: it turned to rich food, rich

food with frills. Instead of the twelve-pound boiled tur-
bot, roast mutton, and suet pudding, it was Turbotin á
la Daumont, Selle d'Agneau Edouard VII, and Bombe
Médicis. *Á la Daumont* means with mushrooms, crayfish, force-meat of whiting, Chablis, and cream; *Edouard
VII* is lined with foie gras and marinaded in Marsala.
Well may we sigh. It is a bit preposterous. But was it, or
was it not, perfect of its kind? I should say sometimes
yes, more often no. Because one trouble with that kind
of cookery is that the effort, the care, the sheer honesty
demanded are more than flesh and blood and avarice can
stand without an occasional recourse to shortcuts,
kitchen aids, the steam table, the bottled essences. I have
dabbled in haute cuisine myself and know; not only that
it takes all day but the kind of day it is. So one does sus-
pect that even in 1910 some of the processes were often
skimped; there must have been already more than a hint
of mass production in the dishing-up of the triple choice
of sixteen courses, particularly in the very large hotels, in
the not-so-large hotels that aped them, and in royal
palaces. The food in these is said to have never been
quite hot. King Leopold I of the Belgians used to rise
from his own table, plate in trembling hand, and shout,
"*La soupe du Roi est froide.*"

What *we* would have found most irksome travelling
fifty years ago were the clothes that went into those
trunks (and had to be put on for dining room and beach),
the starch and studs, the cloth and silk, the *hats*. On every
dressing table in every hotel room was a washing list
printed in five languages:

. . . Jupons/petticoats/unterröcke/enaguas/
sottanini
. . . Gilets blanc/dress waistcoats/weisse westen/
chalecos de etiqueta/panciotti

That. And what went with it. Smoking in the smoking room. Ladies without escorts went in pairs. When
they ordered drink it was in half bottles, preferably
Sauternes; spirits never. To us, with our drip-drys and
quick-drys, our packs of Camels, our mixed rounds of
daiquiris, who have dined in shorts and polo shirt on the
Costa Brava, it would have been intolerable.

There was perhaps after all one golden age of travel.
It was brief, as are such ages, and even while it lasted the
compass was not large. It unfolded during what we now
may see as the early-middle period of the automobile.
The Model T had done its good work and was being left
behind. Balloon tires and self-starters had come in, and
reasonable speeds; comic breakdowns were a thing of the
past. Cars were cheap enough, manageable enough,
worked well enough to be bought and *used* with insou-
ciance. One could take a chum, a girl, a suitcase, set out
on a fine morning, start in the cool of night, *comme le
coeur vous en dise.* . . . Suddenly there was choice; the
world had opened up, even the world twenty miles
beyond one's doorstep. The Iron Horse had abbreviated
the distance between A and B. With the new toys of freedom one could dash to F, see X, dance at Y, and get to B
as well. In its minor way it was a dawn, and to have been
in it, and alive, was good. Less than a hundred years after

Puffing Billy, travel was back again where it began, on the roads. But this time (for a time) with the stings taken out: private, fancy-free—our own.

The 1914 war was over, five years, ten years, fifteen. . . . In Europe the stringencies of social custom had, and remained, slackened. If Maxim's and the Beaurivage Palace still flourished, the traveller also stopped at the Nautique, the Post, the Sol, the Commercio, and the Rendez-Vous des Pêcheurs. The car took him into market towns, to the waterfronts, to the rock pool in the next bay, to the village where they'd found the fresco, into the mountain woods to the inn by the stream. He ate chez Jacques, at the Greek's and chez la Mère Gros, at Luigi's, da Cesare, chez Nine, chez Paul, zum Ochs, at le Bon Coin, and at l'Auberge de la Forêt du Dom. He drank in wine shops and in taverns and in cafés and in cool, dark, narrow, new places called American bars. He sat in the sun and in shade, on city pavements under the chestnut trees, in summer gardens, in piazzas, by lakesides, on quays, below arbors of vine and awnings flapped by mistral, in taprooms redolent of pinewood, and late on terraces above swift nocturnal water. Sometimes there was sawdust under his feet and his elbows touched oilcloth or marble; the napkins were floppy and blue and red, the bottle was brought to him by the patron or a boy or a woman, and the food was the food of the country. Wherever he went he was welcomed, and, within a charmed circle, he went wherever he pleased.

Not for long. The golden circle, never large, narrowed early. The first countries to drop out were the ones struck by phantasmagorical inflations. If it is a rule of golden travel that the living and the moving and the pleasures must be happily within the traveller's means, there is also one that says that the traveller's joys must not be—to any gross degree—at the guest country's expense. He may live off the land only if those who own the land live off it with him. The playground must be a tolerably happy one, and he may only take pleasure, *share* pleasure, where pleasure is, not grab and buy it where it is provided in a vacuum of greed and need. To be a (most likely very profitable) guest who lives more agreeably than he might at home is one thing, and a very nice one too; a difference in degree is a difference in kind. The idyllic traveller cannot be a parasite, a marauder battening on misery; whatever living at the Hotel Adlon for 2/6 a day (including Beluga Malossol and Johannisberger Schloss Spätlese for lunch) may have been, it was not golden travel.

When economics go wrong, politics do not lag far behind. Italy went next. The Blackshirts marched on Rome; the country for all the world remained a travel country—no one who loved Italy could bear to stay away, nor in those days did they stay for long—but it was no more inside the magic circle. Meanwhile, the years were ticking on, whether we knew it or not, ticking on towards 1929, 1933, 1936; towards 1939.

The Wall Street Crash thinned out the travellers themselves; Germany again, and inexorably now, became a condemned playground; the Spanish Civil War broke out; Austria fell. Those who still could travelled all the harder. Where was there to go in those brief last summers? There was Scandinavia, Holland, Switzerland, unfailingly; Greece for a few; there was Yugoslavia; but of the great spellbinders of travel there remained only France. Between the Mediterranean, the Seine, and the Gironde lay the last golden enclosure. It was almost enough.

The French are both soft and stoic. They are above all resilient. Their losses in the 1914 war were on such a tragic scale that it left them with a private and a national sense of irreversible bereavement. If they managed to keep a glow on life it was because of their sensuous vitality, their readiness to enjoy what life had to offer, or what they made it offer; their cultivated and articulate capacity for taking life physically: their passion for food, their due regard for bed, that perennial saving streak that is also an undoing. The French, goodness knows, had plenty of troubles. There was much political bitterness, much corruption, power seeking, distrust, self-interest, ill will, and right-wing and left-wing fanaticism as well as the usual dose of sheer fatuous imbecility. People and parties howled at each other, even shot at each other, as people and parties will when they have nothing total to fear, but as régimes went in Europe the French were bird-free. Their tycoons were as predatory as they come, their budget never balanced; persons who had to live on salaries and pensions were often wretchedly ill off; but a very large number of individual French were comfortable and prosperous and able to stuff themselves, and their mattresses, with paper money in the then still time-honored way of a nation of small shop-

keepers and peasants fattening and selling calves and vegetables for and to each other.

It was the French themselves who in those days discovered what they were quite content to label *le tourisme,*
much in the same way as some twenty years later this sup-
posedly most conservative of people suddenly took to foreign travel. (Before, no sensible French person who could
help it set foot outside the borders, and certainly not in
the name of curiosity or pleasure.) They adored it. They
never stopped talking about it. They doted on everything
that went with it. The roads, the Renaults, the Peugeots,
the Citroëns with the new front-wheel drive cornering
down the N6 at ninety-five an hour, *les voitures améri-
caines (t'as vu la Buick de Jean?),* the mileage, the tree
one nearly went into, the Michelin, the posters (apéritifs
and gasolines), the maps, the road signs (AGINCOURT 5
km), the guidebooks, the mobilo-gastro chatter, the *stops.*
"*On peut déjeuner?*" "*Mais oui, Monsieur—Madeleine:
deux couverts!—vous auriez notre jambon fumé pour com-
mencer avec de la terrine, puis une brandade de morue si
vous la desirez, puis il y a du poulet aux morilles, de la
salade de cressons, du cabécou, de la tarte aux abricots. . . ."*
"*On peut dîner?*" "*Justement ils nous arrivent des lan-
goustes—Gaston: fait voir le 11, une chambre à grand lit—
et ces Monsieur-Dames ont-ils envie de manger du
gibier?*"Ah, the stops—the stops were the heart, the
lifeblood, the marrow, the primum mobile of *le tourisme.*

Everybody had their own place up their sleeve (*allez-
y de ma part*); there were adventurers, dissenters, pio-

neers, but the heavens of the tourist trade moved according to the overall belief in the Michelin Guide's star system— ☆ worth a visit, ☆☆ worth a detour, ☆☆☆ worth the journey. The entire country played at it: what to eat, where to eat, what to drink with what to eat (*quand même pas un Alsace sur la langue de veau!*), what one ate last night, where to eat next Sunday, what one drank, what one paid, what was said: the patron liked to see the customers, the customers liked to see the chef, the sommelier leaned against the table and expressed his views (*un Corton c'est toujours un Corton, mais pour moi le '23 vaut pas le '26*), the brother-in-law would come over for a drink— *on les fait manger; ils nous font manger; on mange. . . .*

AND NOW*—now that we are all so much cannon fodder for the travel industries? Is there anything we can do to improve our regimented lot? Travellers of the World, Unite. You have nothing to lose but your holidays. Well, no one can say that there are not enough of us. (And only so many fine months, so many free days in the year, so many flights, roads, rooms, tables against the wall to go around.) The dice, indeed, are once more loaded. It's a sellers' market. Take it or leave it, and if you don't take it *now* it'll be gone. So in February we buy our tickets for

---

*That *now*—1961—is no longer the now (to become transient in turn) of 2003. It is for the reader to decide what essentially is unchanged and what is changed: changed for better, for worse, for much worse, for monstrous worse. (This note is applicable to much in this book.)

September. Yet the quintessence of good travelling is still freedom. Here today: meet a friend in the square, see a beach, stay on tomorrow. But no: the *reservations.* The Excelsior on the 9th, Stockholm the 12th, Edinburgh . . . Here is where they get us, tied hand and foot, playing our fears (*not* without cause) of finding ourselves without a bed or a booking. It rains in Florence, the galleries for some sprung-up national holiday are going to stay shut, the schedule has us down for another forty-eight hours. We do manage to slip off to Venice on our own; the sun is shining, the food is delicious; why not skip Stockholm this trip? UNI-AIRCRAMP says no. Travellers of the World, Divide. Disperse, narrow your compass, go underground.

It was in that spirit that I decided to make a journey, an unambitious journey, to Italy through France without a timetable or a single reservation. The thing is to choose one's territory (no vast distances, but room to maneuver), get oneself across the Atlantic or the Channel, take a car or hire one, count one's days, and make sure of a booking home. Within that framework, the choice—up to a point!—is ours.

The new day comes when at last our feet are firmly on the continent of Europe and our hands upon the wheel. We may not feel as unworn as Venus risen from the sea, but hope springs eternal. What's behind is behind: the fifty-nine things to do, the getting off. It is at least *possible* to have had a smooth flight from Chicago, to step off bronzed and rested from the SS *Espérance;* the same cannot be said of the various methods of Channel crossings as still practiced. The air-ferries are not bad (if one discounts the ridiculous expense, time, and paper fuss involved in covering twenty-one miles), but they are grounded during every puff of gale or fog. What is wanted of course is not the Tunnel or a Channel bridge but a tunnel *and* a bridge, several tunnels, a whole span of bridges, anchors to make the island know at last its place. The citizens of Calais are said to be preparing for this unlikely event by setting up profitable amenities, but in England it is still looked on as science fiction. Never before in history has England moved as fast as she has been moving backwards in these last few years.

My fellow travellers at the airport (English side) looked shirt-sleeved and dishevelled. Tea slopped in the saucers, ashtrays overflowed, the counters stayed unwiped. The food displayed was predominantly shredded processed cheese on margarine and white. There were also on sale some of those dead-meat pies, the full soggy weight of which has to be eaten to be felt. We stood in line—cheerful—to be served. The service was absent-minded rather than snarling. The beer (it happened to be one of the one hours out of three in which one is allowed to drink some) was, need I say it, warm. My fellow travellers (French side) looked shirt-sleeved and trim. Floors, counters, and glass cases shone with polish. There was Chanel scent for sale. The barman (*clean* white jacket) was not above cutting a slice of ham. There was champagne by the glass. Not very good champagne, but iced and dry. There were also, besides several kinds of French beer, Danish beer, Dutch beer, English beer and stout. The French and Danish beers were chilled, the

Dutch and English cool. Everything cost about twice as much as it did on the other side.

The extreme north of France is not inviting. The country is flat, the roads uneven and impeded by level crossings, good places to stop at few; it is as if the population could hardly wait to be rid of the new-landed visitors and get on with their drab agriculture of turnip and sugar beet. My own idea was down to Rouen, quickly, and a very good lunch. The first. Luncheon on the quay, of mussels and sole. The choice, I said, would be ours. True enough, if ours includes the car's. Bad cars break down, good cars exercise a subtler despotism. Nothing, no death rattle of a poor old crock, is as compelling as the moral blackmail levied by a new car. Mine, as expressed by its glossy service manual, had to have a special oil changed for another very special oil at a certain number of miles. That number was up *now*. The manual also informed one where this operation had best be executed in this part of the world. Accordingly I headed to a not very attractive town in the Department of the Somme. The garage was in the dingy but machine-loud outskirts where such establishments are usually to be found. A number of namesakes of my car were standing about in various stages of disembowelment. The mechanics had not finished their lunch; I had not begun mine. It is my habit, however, to carry iron rations. The manager's wife invited me to a chair in her kitchen, spotless and somnolent. I unwrapped what I could. Danish rye, a hunk of cheddar, eggs. Iron was the word. The woman eyed me like something in the zoo.

"*Vous êtes danoise?*" she said.

I denied this.

Her eyes stayed on the bread; when she saw how black it was, she squealed. I explained that in my opinion the bread in England was not fit to eat.

"You come from Denmark?" she said.

I said that Danish bread was to be had in London like Camembert and Bombay duck. "*C'est* noir," she said. I dared her to eat a piece; she shrank with giggles; further communication failed.

I spent that first night in Normandy at a place that is rather typical of one new kind of French country hotel. It is the converted small château or manor house, converted with taste and perhaps not quite enough money spent on the plumbing, and run with only relative amateurishness by people not originally brought up to the trade. This particular one, standing in beautifully kept grounds, is an eighteenth-century house overhanging a small green-banked river. The French lay much stress on reception, *l'accueil*, and it is accorded special marks in their many guidebooks. Quite rightly so. The tone, the level of intelligence, of the welcome, the speed with which the traveller is enabled to put his car at rest and find himself *with* his belongings behind a shut door and *alone*, makes all the difference at that weary hour.

I am not prejudiced in favor of Normandy. In winter it is bleak, in summer pretty. Anyone inalienably attached to the Mediterranean landscapes, to olive and ilex, to the bleached bare spaces of Provence and the terraced Tuscan hills, is not captivated long by hedgerows and apple trees.

Normandy is a cider, not a wine, region, which makes for a broody, sullen, suicidal form of drunkenness. But cider and calvados are innocuous compared to the Norman affluence of butter and cream. Eating, overeating, is not always the amiable weakness we like to think it: gluttony and rapacity often go hand in hand. Cream and butter are quite literally the Normans' Golden Calf. During the Occupation even one-cow farmers grew to Cadillac riches from black-market butter, and so in 1944 the populace threw stones at the advancing Allied soldiers because liberation from the Germans put an end to that.

The *accueil* at that Norman hotel was perfect. Entering my room was like walking into a Monet painting: the window *was* the river, and one might almost touch the live, leaf-reflecting water. Alas, as I knew before the night was out, the room was also damp, and there were many serious things wrong with the woodwork, the pipes, the flooring. . . . This is not a complaint, only a statement of the facts of life. One cannot have everything. Old houses such as these can only be lived in as they are or destroyed; to do them over at impossible expense would put an end to them as twelve-roomed hotels. A matter of choice.

We (I had been joined by friends from Paris) went down to dinner. The menu was large, that is, it was on a large sheet of cardboard. I watched out for the cream. It *was* in evidence. But looked at as a whole that menu was sound and unpretentious: two made dishes, one of chicken, one of duck; red meat grilled to order; fresh trout, lobster, also cooked to order; and that, with a terrine, one soup, vegetables, and some puddings, was the lot. The chicken, a *spécialité de la maison* of course, was simply a good deal of white chicken (a decently bred fowl) presented with mushrooms and a sauce stiff with cream (not flour) flavored with calvados; it was one of those foolproof dishes doted on by the French because they are so rich and by Anglo-Saxons because they seem so hard to get at home. I doted on them myself until I was about twenty-five. This one was as good as they can be. The entrecôte I had was a thick cut of first-rate meat—firm texture, well flavored—it was properly grilled and served with a large piece of butter (nothing amiss with the quality) and fresh watercress. The fried potatoes were burning to the fingers, slender and crisp, and left no trace of grease. The balance was marred by the *haricots verts,* brown-green and softened into a blotter for butter, a standard treatment of vegetables in France.

Wine. It much depends on who does the buying with what standards and from whom. Do the patron and his wife know their stuff, or do they order according to the blandishments of the shipper's salesman? It takes a lot to keep a fair wine list. As for the customer, there is no longer such a thing as a *safe* wine. Those Anglo-Saxons who are wine drinkers are usually spoilt because standards of export are high. Transport and duty costing what they do, it is foolish to ship muck across the seas. I drink better claret in England than I can hope to find during a casual trip through France. There, the home market is so huge—in the one street in Paris where I usually stay there are a dozen people, five of them women, who are known to drink up to their ten liters of red a day—and has become so indiscriminate that cheap production for high yield, inferior grapes, inexpert handling, and adulteration pay.* This goes for the *ordinaires,* the current wines, splashed out by the liter, as well as for the named and bottled mainstays of good daily drinking: the Anjous, Beaujolais, Bordeaux Blancs, and Médocs Supérieurs; the Grands-Crus, real ones, are still to be found—at a price—and in Paris, Nice, and Bordeaux as well as in Boston, London, Brussels, San Francisco. We stuck to the mainstays, and were lucky. A Muscadet without sharpness, a passable Châteauneuf. It is not hard really to tell sound wine—your insides, from five minutes to the morning after, are the judge.

The coffee, too, was fair (they still *will* mess with those filters). They tipped us with liqueurs. We chose calvados; it did not make us sullen. To sum up, the place was good of its kind. By other standards, those of very expensive London restaurants or the run of reputed Paris restaurants or those of some famed places on the tourist routes, the quality and honesty of the cooking and materials here, the individual attention, were remarkable. What keeps it so? The right patron (some people like to give their best; others are born cheaters), discriminating customers, competition. Outside the summer and the Easter seasons there is not much transient trade (foreign transients seldom praise and never complain); the backbone are regulars, local families eating out, Sunday Parisians, people who will come again *or* stay away. In this

---

* *Not* so now: one marked change for the better.

fertile valley it is but a stone's throw to the next *spécial-ité de la maison*.

Full marks, too, for the get-off. We decided on an early start, a very early start. You don't have to break it to them, *they* put it to you: Breakfast—six o'clock? seven o'clock? ten o'clock? Miserable hours for the staff? Not at all. Madame is up on her own, bent over a gas-ring in her dressing gown. Tea, coffee, or chocolate in piping jugs, hot croissants from the baker, honey, two kinds of jam. I am not mentioning the other stuff. The bill is ready too, and there is change. Not a small bill, but expectedly so, and scrupulous. The car is still waiting under the trees, unlocked. Nobody has touched the luggage.

One good way to drive down to the South of France, if one wants to avoid the overcrowded and overpriced National roads No.'s 7 and 6, and I always do except in the dead of winter and a great hurry, is to go roughly by Chartres, Blois, Bourges (or through the Loire), Moulins, or Montluçon, through the Auvergne, over the Cévennes and into the Ardèche by Clermont-Ferrand, Le Puy, and come out into the Rhône Valley anywhere between Valence and Avignon. The roads, like pretty nearly all first and secondary roads in France, are very good and except for the Sunday-luncheon traffic half empty most of the year. Getting south takes a bit longer, but only if you count in hours, as there is rather more winding and climbing and the road often passes through villages, but the actual mileage is the same. The country is varied and most beautiful, and there are of course a great many things to see. The Auvergne alone, to mention only the less obvious, is rich in Romanesque churches of astonishing originality, the painted basilica at Issoire, Auzon, Brioude, Fontannes, the stupendous Benedictine abbey on top of a rock at La Chaise-Dieu. . . . But I am concerned here with the material framework of travel, not its contents.

The Auvergne is another region of abundance; mountainous, well to the south of center, it is still cow pasture (blue cheese, Cantal) and also swarms with pigs, barnyard fowls, game birds, and sturdy vines.

We stopped at an inn near Riom, a charming place, a traditional establishment of the old school (beds provided so that those who dine may sleep) and starred by Michelin. That system flourishes as much as ever. Meals in such places are set meals; you *can* eat à la carte, there's nothing inflexible about arrangements, but somehow you never do as well. The form is three set meals, three menus: *Le Menu à 7NF, Le Menu à 16NF,* and *Notre Menu Gastronomique.* Before looking at any, you know that you will have to take the sixteen-franc one. The cheap menu will have been made to appear so unexciting, so mingy (by contrast), that you feel you cannot bear to dine off just soup, omelette, lamb chops, salad, ice cream; while the gastronomic one is sheer show-off, a shop window, not designed for human consumption. Besides, it costs thirty-two Nouveaux Francs, c/s/b (cover/service/drink) *not* included. So you also shy from *Les Délices des Anges—Le Pintadeau Entier Sous Cloche* (2 Pers.)—*Le Soufflé G'd-Marnier* (40 mins), and get down to business. The manageable menu offered us a choice between something hot in pastry and two pâtés. We chose—being two at that stage—one *terrine de canard* and one *pâté de gibier*. The range of quality in pâtés is wide; at the extreme ends of the scale they have nothing in common but a name. These were far removed from the starchy-filler and gray-pulp variety, and they were served as they should be, not on a little plate with a tired leaf but in their earthen terrines left on the table with a good knife, plenty of hot toast, and bread. It is easiest to say what a good pâté should not be—fat, too close or gelatinous in texture, too salty, underseasoned, all peppercorns and gristle, overherbed, soused in cheap brandy, stale, too high, too fresh, worst of all not made of plenty of sound meat. Ours were none of these things: they were made of duck and pork and hare and couldn't have tasted better.

On arriving I had asked for some white wine to drink, and they had given me a glass of a local one to try. I liked it and ordered a half bottle for apéritif, and it went on drinking itself well. It was a most pleasant discovery. The name is St-Pourçain, it was fairly dry and not a bit thin, one could feel at once that it was wholesome, and it had that fleeting taste of earth and fruit and flint that one loves to catch in a white wine. I have since learnt that it can be got in London but have not had the heart to try. Here it costs 3F. 60 a bottle, restaurant price. We ordered some more with our terrines and the second course, which was either trout or *Lotte à l'Américaine*. I don't think trout out of a tank is worth eating because its muscles and so its flesh will have gone flabby, while trout straight out of a cold river is so good that it should be had by itself, in suitable quantities, with melted butter and perhaps some boiled potatoes, and not shoved between two high-flavored courses, so we chose the *lotte*, a fish* that ought to be able to stand up to the *américaine* treatment: cayenne pepper, tomato concentrate, herbs, flared brandy. . . . The dish that arrived was not quite like that; the sauce that covered it was thickened with starch (gluey) and had a smooth brown uniformity that betrayed a semi-mass-produced origin in a stock saucepan. Next (with *red* St-Pourcain, nicely robust and no disappointment) one of us had chicken done with morels under a bubbling crust: a bit of a virtuoso dish but neatly turned out, and the morels, the firm black nightshade so like a species of sea fauna in appearance, with the hot white chicken and their compounded essences was delicious.

The alternate main course, irresistibly described as *Jambon sous la cendre*, was a comedown. Whatever merits the ham may have possessed were smothered under not hot ashes but a drenching of our old acquaintance the smooth brown sauce, gingered on this time by a lacing of Madeira—cooking Madeira; no other is purveyed in the French provinces. There came also a panful of new potatoes right off the stove in their parsley and butter; these were pure and good and horribly out of place. What was wanted if anything was a spoonful of plain rice. (Which the French mysteriously are unable to make. A pilaf, just; *à l'impératrice*, yes; plain steamed rice, never.) Salad, dressed to order—cheeses—fruit—fruit tarts and ices for

---

*Our new friend, the monkfish.

those who wanted them—the filters—a presentation bottle. . . . The place indeed had many virtues: everything set
before us had been in most generous amounts, to me an
essential for good faith. They were very friendly, commercial friendliness, but dispensed with good nature; the
bill was moderate. Two-thirds or less than it would have
been in Normandy, or the Côte d'Azur for that matter,
and this holds good for most of provincial France off the
main tourist track.

I went into the details of this dinner because it was so
typical of both the good things and the defects one may
expect to find elsewhere. Nearly everywhere we went, we
found the same inequality: one dish outstanding, the next
a travesty. Much of French cooking is based on methods
that mean long, slow work by hand. There aren't enough
people anymore to do it, nor is it economical; the family
may help, but the family may not be numerous or may
have other ideas for themselves. Not every young man,
even in the Dordogne, will want to spend his life stirring
sauce grand-veneur. At the same time, it's a question of
prestige and prejudice. The French still *believe* in sauces.
If it's without a sauce, or not flamed or puffed, or encased
in crust or wrapped or stuffed with something else, it may
be very good—it may be a great deal *better*—but it's not
la cuisine. La cuisine was (*is,* they would say) one of the
glories of France. Nobody else knows anything: the Italians live on macaroni, the Germans on potatoes; the English cook exclusively in tepid water; the Americans do not
cook at all. French cookery stands like an aging beauty—
forward ho, nobody is going to notice the little bit of

rouge and dye, nobody is going to notice the little bouillon cube.

How did I fare in general? As far as hotels went, very well. We drove across the Rhône and back into the mainstream, spent some days at Aix, a week between Bandol and Nice. Easter came and went. We did not sleep in the car, nor in the cold-water pension, nor on the billiard table in the station hotel. (I am now convinced that this free-wheeling is perfectly practicable ten months of the year for anyone unencumbered by small children. Only July and August need a different approach.) French hotels are getting better and better. The really monstrous plumbing of my golden youth is giving way to tiled and glistening shower-baths and WCs. You may even wash these days with comfort and hot water at some gas stations. (The discrepancy between the near Swiss domestic cleanliness of the French and the filth of their public places has always puzzled me.) Nor are hotel rooms expensive; in fact, they cost less than anywhere else in Europe except Portugal, but of course the bill catches up with one on the food. And the food, after the first flush of arrival, all too often fails to stand up. Great pretensions breed great expectations. I recall some nadirs: the starred *auberge* where at least three courses of the dinner were built around batter—fishy fritters, pancakes encasing béchamel and cheese, pancakes encasing béchamel and vanilla essence—and where the wine pressed upon one was an acrid rosé in a dolled-up bottle. The well-frequented place not far from Cannes where the red mullet was not fresh and the *escalopes* had been precooked and reheated (the first *can* happen; the second is pre-meditated). The famous restaurant by the sea where the dinner produced for us—a table of four—was so shocking that I prefer to believe that it can only have been due to a chain of chance mishaps. The disgraceful rotgut served without batting an eyelid by far too many places in the South, and about which one can do nothing, as the "better wines" in such places are sure to be neither well chosen nor well kept. And yet at times one does eat beautifully in the Midi, as indeed one should. I remember an hors-d'oeuvres of home-cured small black olives, anchovy, firm butter, and radishes just pulled from the earth. I remember sardines grilled dripping from the sea; a little dish of veal cooked with new artichokes and sorrel. Striped bass, fish soup, *oursins*. A stew of wild boar, rabbit done with peppers in a flat black pan at a Spanish place at Aix, green almonds, the first apricots, a round, hard goat cheese eaten with fresh figs and the red Rhône Gigondas. Other wines, obscure and world-travelled: Château Simone, grown in upper Provence; Cassis, still one of the best of oyster wines, but beware, there is not much of it, and not all of its shippers are true; a nice natural tough red wine made by a peasant near St Tropez and a nice natural white wine made by a peasant near Grasse; a vintage champagne light like fine silk; and a sequence of exquisite wines at a luncheon given by an American woman. I even remember *one* meal at a star place where the whole menu was held in impeccable bounds and was from first fork to last spoonful delicious. It was a Friday, and we ate *maigre*. We (a party) began with a salmon from the Loire accompanied by the lightest cucumber mayonnaise, a coolness of pink and pale green; the central dish was simply a hot stew of seafood, and it was as good as it sounds.

The French are prosperous again—*ça marche*—and the young, disillusioned or not, feel free. People probably work less, care less. . . . They certainly earn more, drink more; standards are lower, workmanship more shoddy, the new *things* look hideous, but the people look thriving. Virtual dictatorship, near police state, plastic-bomb throwing—the general political precariousness of the country is hair-raising, but then whose is not? The French dash off for their *vacances*, pour into the Midi: there is an exhilarating vitality at large, and with it a sense of live and let live, of individual ease, and it stays with one from border to border.

LET US LOOK AT ITALY. If one were wafted straight from our shores onto the Via Aurélia at Ospedaletti (ROMA = 676 km), our first shock of pleasure might be the cypresses and fig trees, the pink-and-blue-washed houses, the dazzling sea. When the transition is made by motoring in from France, the first shock is the mad driving. It is driving that scares the French. Each time, one finds that it has got more impossible. It is not that Italian driving does get worse; it stays the same, and they drive very well, extremely well, too well, every man boy jack of them; it is that each year there are more cars to drive. Italian motoring is like the nationalism of a very young nation, but there is more to it than that; there is also a natural affinity: the automobile must be God's special gift to the Italians. He even created it noisy. The Fiat, the Lancia, the Alfa are the young man's fine feathers; at the wheel, he is a bird of paradise displaying a dance of courtship—love my car, love me. Courtship in the animal kingdom is competition. So it's a battlefield. On narrow roads. Plenty of blind corners. And precipices. Tanks, too: double-decker buses, oil trucks triple-linked.

One gets used to it. To the point of feeling dazed by the slow pace during the first hour out of Italy. But one never gets used to the coast road between Nice and Pisa. From the frontier to Genoa, squeezed between the Sea-Alps and the sea, twined with a busy railway, tunnelled, quarried, tram-lined, the road is frustrating and murderous. Once again one swears to oneself that next time one will come in by way of Switzerland and Milan. At Alassio, we stopped to break the tension. Alassio has pretty arcaded streets full of those shops where they will make you a pair of sandals or a silk shirt in twenty minutes, and for the Riviera it has a good beach. We found that it had become a German enclave. Things are like that in Italy (an *occuppée* mentality formed by history: layers of soft yielding, nonchalant compliance, below bedrock). Florence used to be English (when we were still able to spread ourselves), the Americans have chosen Rome, Venice is an international city; the Germans, a modest choice one must say, have taken over Alassio. I am not distressed by the sight of a good many people on a holiday. People must go somewhere; there are only so many places in the sun; that we *are* so many is not the fault of these actual generations; I hope they, we, will all enjoy ourselves. What does distress me are the unbecoming, commercial, but stupid commercial, monkey tricks practiced by the natives. God knows the French are great tourist-trappers, but they have kept some dignity. Look at this Italian in his doorway, waving a napkin, "Nicy spaghetti!"; he is behaving like a *silly* prostitute. Alassio is plastered with notices in German touting *asti spumante* and whipped cream, misspelled, grotesquely worded, as if they had been taught by some tipsy joker in the small hours, as in fact they very likely were. And so, in English, in French, in anything, is the whole of Italy; it's the new polyglot illiteracy. The grammar or lack of it doesn't matter, not a scrap, only the fact that the people who utter those invitations turn themselves into parrots, cut the link between thought and speech. . . .

When Italian food shops are good, which they are in all the towns and all the resorts of the North and Center, they are very very good. To me the first one after absence is almost unbearable. The cleanness, the smell of Parma ham and sometimes of truffle, the order, the reasoned abundance—I am moved to transports of appreciation. Look at the whole cheeses in their beautiful black rinds, look at the hanging provolone, the *fiaschi,* the salami; they *have* fresh *fior di latte and mascarpone*; the cooked ham looks good too, and the tunny fish. . . . But I buy our picnic with restraint. *Prosciutto di montagna,* smoky and mild; a few olives; bread, not the rolls, which are often sad stuff, but a cut of a coarse baked loaf; a wedge of parmesan, the hard *grana*: a morsel is prized off and tendered on the tip of the knife—yes, this one; and one soft cheese, a ball of mozzarella.

Cherries off a stall in the street. A wine shop. What they chiefly drink here comes from Piedmont and the Val d'Aosta just above, Barbera and Barbaresco, frank reds, rather strong. I take a flask of the lighter Bardolino from the Veneto because it is an agreeable wine to drink. The good wines of Italy are easy and companionable. Soave, the undenatured Chiantis, Valpolicella, Bardolino, the rosé from Ravello . . . You can do with them what you never would with a hock or claret, trundle them about in the car, opened and all, fling in a handful of ice, drink them without a glass, drink them at all hours, with any food, in carefree quantities.

After Genoa the road rises, the curves sharpen, the traffic becomes *more* lively; from now until La Spezia one forgets about the frustration and concentrates on the murderous. In between, we spent the night at Portofino. This is now one of the most, probably the most, expensive places on the entire Mediterranean coast between Torremolinos and Maratea. (There are 1,051 inhabitants, and 1,039 of them are said to have each tucked away the equivalent of ten thousand American dollars in the last few years.) These few feet of land between hill and sea could not be more fashionable or overrun. Which only goes to show what good taste people have. For that constellation of harbor, small township, and castello is ravishing, and remains so, as the law forbids anyone to alter so much as the shape of a window. When we were there it was out of season and in moonlight; one cannot ask for more.

We dined. The first dinner in Italy—will it stand up? is anything ever as good as one remembers? It did, and it was. We ate a light curled pasta that lay like a nest on the plate, with the green Genoese dressing of pounded basil and garlic, and then we ate a firm grilled fish, a sea bream, charred and nutty, seasoned only with a thread of limpid Tuscan olive oil and some lemon. With it we drank the wine of the neighborhood, white Cinqueterre I had never had before, and it was most pleasant. Later on the waiter made us a salad of young sprigs and leaves, a salad such as you can get only in Italy, and in Italy only in the spring. Then there was fruit, and cheese, melting *stracchino* and parmesan full-flavored and crumbly, and with these we drank each a quartino of Valpolicella. Everything tasted simple and strong. Everything had been made honestly, quickly, without frills, but as it should be. It was whole-some, life-giving. . . . We had eaten well; we felt well. As we sat in the piazza inhaling our black half inches of dou-ble espressi, I felt very happy.

After Portofino one comes a bit down to earth. Not for long, though. One is soon at Pisa. Who—however road-worn, tired, outraged by his last encounter with a Vespa—can forbear from feeling a pang of childlike pleas-ure at the sight of that extraordinary assemblage of felic-itous architectural absurdities standing on that tidy strip of grass?

I have often slept at Pisa, in comfort and in squalor, but I can't say I have ever eaten very well. My luck and fault entirely. Restaurants in Italy all look much the same, so if one's not tipped off one knows it may be hit or miss. Putting one's nose inside helps, but that needs the resolution to walk out again. A place being half empty is no indication either way; the inhabitants of Cremona may not stir out on Mondays or after eight P.M. Of course there are the guidebooks, even Michelin now, but by the time a place gets into one it often has already passed its prime. The kind of integrity that makes Italian cooking is built largely on innocence and popular eating habits; it tends to go off when confronted by foreigners and success. Not that you can go so terribly far wrong; you will always eat. The Italian range is not so very large, excellence at one end (an excellence achieved by texture, the goodness of materials and their startling freshness), innocuous dullness at the other. The worst you can expect is a bellyful of ready-made spaghetti followed by a pallid bit of veal. I've lived in Italy off and on since I was a child, I've had some starkly bare food in the poor south and in other remote places, but never once in my memory have I been given something that had gone bad (a very common experience elsewhere), nor can I recall any outstanding instance of *grande cuisine manquée* even in the internationally minded hotels.

I forgot: there *is* a skeleton in the culinary cupboard, and it is made of fishbone. It is the national illusion about the fish soup, *il cacciucco*. They love it, they drive miles to the Ligurian waterfronts to order it, they even think they can eat it. The Italian fish soup has been described for all time in its crazy glory by Norman Douglas in *Siren Land,*

and I can only say here that the soup is all he says it is—fishes' heads, coruscating color, overpowering spices, spikes, sharp little bones, and uncrackable little crabs—and that the serving of it still flourishes.

After Leghorn we dawdled down the straightened coast road towards Rome, half-consciously postponing an arrival that to me is always tinged with awe, looking at Etruscan tombs, stopping here and there, at Castiglione della Pescaia, at Porto Ercole. . . . In Italy when the weather is right it is joy itself; when it fails the single wet day is dismal and dead; just so, existence in this unique country is at times Elysian and at others like a sojourn inside a power-driven mincing machine. Like other travellers, we were alternately floating along in elated bliss or reeling off the streets felled by combat fatigue. There are always marvels, always pinpricks. . . . Here stands Diana's temple; it is a private moment: *"Postacards? Cartes postales?"* The uninvited guide continues at your heels, talking, talking, you do not want to mar the day by the loud word that may even fail to send him off. You turn into the Square, the Palazzo Pubblico, a first glimpse of arches, colonnades . . . you stop to park the car: from the curb there rise four human leeches.

The best of coffees is yours everywhere for the price of three or four of those light new coins. You sit down; order an ice, too, with a swirl of cream; the radio, off-station, starts ablast; behind you begins a glissade of kitchen plates.

The noise! There are no two ways about it, either you are Italian or Italian-built and don't hear it, or you are not and you do and it is unbearable. Scooters revving, motor horns, open exhausts, female lungs, a steam drill, canned music, and nimble hammers pounding on sound steel—shuddering noises, fine noises, honest noises, noises for noise's sake, from the backyard, from next door, from the cinema, from the café, from the street . . .

Italians, for all their happy gregariousness, seem to do things best individually. One houseboy and the house is kept scrubbed, polished, in beautiful order, the marketing is done, drinks served, delicious meals appear, the guests' luggage is gently taken down, disposed of in the car. All this with calm, the unobtrusive smile. Two boys: voices raised, dithering to and fro, a tug over each suitcase—off flies the handle—general agitation. Three boys: a crowd. What traveller has not been the center of these tussles, at the station, the taxi rank, leaving a hotel, trying to take a boat? It is wearing to be put into the position of the Solomonic baby several times a day.

Fifty million Italians do not make so much a democracy as Disraeli's Two Nations. Italy, too, or most of it, is prospering. The well-to-do are doing extremely well; the poor are much less poor and some of them beginning to be even decently well off. But the dividing chasm is still there, tangibly and intangibly, in education, in civic and political responsibility—the poor are the wards, the others not the guardians but just privileged citizens—to a diminishing extent in dress, and most decisively in the outlook of the two sides themselves and in the outlook of the Church. Such division—among many other things—is limiting; it stunts evolution, growth. The haves are almost pushed into cynicism and frivolity; the poor stay blocked in their sphere: work, frugality, acceptance (or rebellion), ducking under the bureaucratic snares, the family, the day and what it brings, enjoyment, zest for life, getting *on* with it. Admirable, much of it, but is it enough? And on top of it all are the foreigners streaming in, and who are they, all rich of course, incomprehensible, alien in their virtues and their ways, another species; the Church insinuates that they are outside the pale—no stockings in church, sunbathing, smoking women—again it does not help. So in the end modern Italy is really split in three—the rich, the poor, and the tourists.

ROME. It is a name so potent, a spell so great. Rome, the most superb of the live hunting grounds of magic, the seat of the gods and man, the capital of pleasure, a feast to the eye, to memory, to all the senses . . . Love renders mute. I cannot write of Rome; it is far beyond my powers. Anyhow, Rome is there to be plunged into, to be believed. You walk in Rome, you eat, you see, you sniff, if it comes at all it will come to you in that way. But here again, this is no longer true; we are up against the facts of modern life—can one still walk, can one still *move, breathe?* No longer in Rome: the cars and their fumes fill everywhere, stagnant, solid, or moving at mowing speed. Every crossing is a hazard, every outing an ordeal. The Piazza San Pietro is a car park, Bernini's façade disfigured by a hundred excursion buses. The traffic in Rome has attained nightmare dimensions; it is not too much to say that this is a tragedy.

To the many of us whose love of Italy was instilled early, the very thought of the incomparable beauty and riches of Italian art and the Italian countryside has been a solid possession, an inexhaustible promise of a perennial inheritance to come into, to explore more deeply with time and a mellowing mind; but already today physical existence in the larger towns of Italy is viable only for the tough and the young. What's to become of it all? If we are not going to blow up our planet, we are going to ruin it by our numbers and our wheels. Everywhere there is galloping up on us the same new story, before we have been able to grasp, before we have learnt how, or even decided to cope: overpopulation. Too many sheep in the pen. And with it, decline in the quality of living, frustration of spontaneity, universal dullness.

Let us turn to more manageable aspects; let us turn once more to the pleasures that are undiminished: one eats in Rome as well as one ever did. The half-dozen or so places with the now international reputations are doing fine; if some of them have become a bit more furbished and a good bit more crowded and high priced, the food is still first rate, and for each of them there has sprung up round the corner, in the next street, across the river maybe, an old trattoria on the way up, getting a new name. It will be discovered, enjoyed, praised, written up, crowded into, redecorated (here always the last step but one), and replaced. A healthy state. I dined out every night I could, and each time I went home more than pleased. That is not the case with all travellers in Italy, and I think that questions of taste apart, it's a matter of ordering. If the restaurants look much alike, the menus, too, read much the same. This means little. One should choose from what one sees exhibited proudly on the table coming in—the dish of new shelled peas, the coiled fresh pasta, the trussed birds, stuffed peppers, salad bowls, wild strawberries—and according to what one feels like eating. There are some prawns, the waiter proposes them grilled, one is hungry, could one not have a risotto of seafood? Certainly, if one is willing to wait twenty minutes (while eating something else), and now is the time to say *how* one would like the risotto made. They expect it. Creamy? on the mild side? or with plenty of saffron and spice? The French would send you packing. Here, nearly everything can be ordered as you like it: boiled, fried, grilled, hot or cold, in butter, in oil, without fat, in batter, without sage, without Marsala, with garlic, with an egg. . . . Nor is it *necessary* to begin a meal with spaghetti. I happen to be fond of nearly every form of pasta; I like it with bacon and red peppers, I like it with young green peas, with chopped ham and cream, with filets of fresh tomato, or *in bianco* just plain with butter and cheese. I like tagliatelle, taglioline, fettucine, cappellini, lasagne, farfalle, parpadelle, tonnellini. I like rice, I like gnocchi, polenta, cannelloni, and pasticci, but if I did not, I could spend a month on end in Italy without having to touch *pasta asciutta* for any course. Well, what else *is* there?

There is ham, salami, smoked ham, melon, figs, fresh mozzarella or ricotta, anchovy, tunny fish, artichokes hot or cold, *finocchi,* chickpeas in oil, salt cod, *vitello tonnato,* quail, soups, cream soup, clear soup, chicken broth done with any garnish, omelettes, flat stuffed omelettes, truffles in cheese, truffles in egg, small marrow, spinach crusted with parmesan, asparagus, peas with ham, little hot dishes of sweetbreads, or of eggplant and bubbling cheese, mushrooms, *gamberi* and scampi, *frittura,* anything you wish with a mayonnaise, and about three dozen varieties of fish.

When it comes to the main course, ask again, ask to see the meat, the new catch—it will be brought to you with pleasure—pick out your lobster, choose your cut. Never get discouraged by the menu; never eat at places that have menus written in English like this:

scalope bolognese style	* scalope pleasure style
scalope according	* meagre of scalope
Arrosteds	* paste & bean
Humids	* foot & bean
Fritters	
green from season	

Some highlights: white truffles grated at the table over a plate of very fine egg pasta (Rome, Turin). Pilaf of prawn and mussels (Venice). Pasta of a kind that puts it in a class apart (Bologna, Rome, Milan). *Gran Bollito,* boiled beef, veal, fowl, sausage, and tongue (Piedmont, Rome). *Bistecca alla fiorentina* (Florence, Rome). Young vegetables and primeurs (Rome, Naples, Florence). Rare salad greens (Florence). Mozzarella, the dawn-made buffalo cheese dripping with its own milk (the south). Wild asparagus, apricots, melon, figs, peaches, grapes.

Some stand-bys and good things: hams, smoked meats. Thick soups. The bean dishes of Tuscany. The larger sea fish, *orata dentice*, *spigola*, *san pietro*, swordfish, fresh tunny, also soles, red mullet, and some of the small fry. Veal kidneys, *fegato alia veneziana*. Boiled chicken, boiled beef. *Ossobuco*, *stufato*, spiced sausage. Most of the short orders of veal, *saltimbocca*, *involtini*, *milanese*. Baked lamb (good sometimes); the fillets of turkey and chicken. Broiled Tuscan chicken. *Melanzane*, *fagiolini*, zucchini. Fave off the pod. All salads. The taste of the tomatoes. The olive oils. Ten cheeses. The pastry in the larger towns. Sicilian oranges.

Some things to avoid: game birds as currently done— preroasted, overcooked, smothered in sage, and reheated. *Pasta pronta*—nine times out of ten, soft-flour spaghetti kept warm, dished up with tomato and meat sauce. Pizza (nearly always). Most restaurant roasting. Rosemary, apt to protrude like too many pine needles from an overwhelmed bit of pork. Thin, insipid puddings like *zuppa inglese*. The open white wines dispensed in Rome. Pasteurized Chianti, dead in the glass. Wine in fancy bottles.

Two postscripts for dispelling gloom. To make certain of some swimming (in early May) we went south below Salerno, into the Mezzogiorno. After a short initial streak of foul weather, it got hot; it was summer. Drawn by the pleasures of discovery, we drove down well into Calabria. How easy it is now. When I was a child much of it was malaria country, and I remember being hurried away from Paestum before sundown; even a few years ago casual travel was not to be undertaken lightly because there was hardly anywhere to sleep. Now there is a network of Jolly Hotels and Autostelle—motels, run (well) by the Automobile Club of Italy. There is also a chain of the new Agip gas stations (the centipedal dog), which sport showers, coffee bars, and luncheon counters, so that one is now most competently and cleanly lodged and looked after in the deep South. The beaches are unbelievable: wide, long, white, and empty. There is fishing. The roads are good; the countryside is as beautiful as a dream, untouched, unspoilt; the people friendly, with a grave archaic grace, the open hand raised to greet the stranger.

The last lap, Florence. We had three days. While the sun was up we pressed in rush-hour crowds through the Uffizi galleries, the Pitti, the Bargello, across the Ponte Vecchio. . . . At night we ate. There was a back-street place I knew in the old days. It had two bare tables in a sort of hallway to a smoke-filled kitchen into which one squeezed, first come, first served. It was always hot and hellishly noisy, and afterwards the stink of burnt meat lingered in one's clothes for a week. The customers were Florentine workmen and aristocracy, smart professional men and paunchy visiting Milanese. The benches were hard and narrow and not provided with backs, the service rough and none too ready, and at one time of the evening this broiling cage would be invaded by an itinerant band. One endured it because of the food. The food was superb. The best of its kind in Europe.

We arrived. The queue stretched halfway down the street: Italian sports cars, a Mercedes, American limousines. Italians in evening clothes and diamonds, Americans bristling with the less obvious exterior signs of wealth. Everybody stood and waited for about three-quarters of an hour. The cage was just the same: nothing had changed, the benches, the service, the din, the smoke from the charcoal fires. In due course we ate. We ate birds off a spit and a plate of Florentine grass, the whole white of a chicken in foaming butter out of a little battered aluminum pan such as I have never eaten and shall never eat elsewhere; we ate steak, wild asparagus, strawberries. The red wine was delicious. We paid as we went out—there were no menus—the prices, too, were unchanged. It had never been for nothing, it was not so now, but for what we had been given we had been made a present.

The second night I tried to get to a place that had been described to me in Rome as the heir apparent to our No 1. It has no name. What it says over the door is simply TRATTORIA. As it happens the street, a streetlet, is unnamed too. The directions I had been given sounded like an incantation: stand with your back to the fountain, face such a bridge, count twenty paces to the west. . . . It worked. I found it.

A back room attached to a kitchen, bare communal tables, benches, cool scowls for welcome, crowded to overflowing, but no queue. No diamonds, no foreigners, no Giuliettas. The customers: Florentine aristocracy and workmen with a sprinkling of professional men. Good bread, olive oil, bowls of grated cheese, fresh-cut lemons, and good young wine in profusion on the table. We ate *cecci, baccalà,* grilled chicken, beefsteak, garden asparagus, *grana,* raspberries. It was superb. We paid as we walked out; the bill was small.

The third night we set out for a place known to a local friend. It went by a nickname. Same décor, same initial lack of cordiality (they all warm up when you've had something to eat). The customers: workmen, clerks, petty officials. We ate boiled beef and fave, we ate a savory mince, a thick grilled fillet of veal with hot asparagus, green almonds, *mascarpone,* and wood strawberries. Decent wine flowed. Nothing could have been better. As we left we paid, and the sum was ludicrous. I put down the address; in a couple of years it will be spelled out for the asking by the head porters of the Excelsior and the Grand—the third in line for the carriage trade. Long may they all flourish.

THE ANCHOR AND
THE BALLOON

A Diary in Switzerland 1953

⌒ SATURDAY, AUGUST 1ST. Morning. Stepped off the train, still trailing a little sand, by the door swung shut last night on the platform at Cannes, funnelled through the passage of the double customs—Douane Française, other colors, a common language, a different design of caps, Douane Suisse—followed the unhurried porter's trolley to the cloakroom down the kiosked hall, and walked, free for a space of hours between a choice of trains, into the spacious, sparkling, luxurious town, pouring with light, ablaze with water, snow-lit above the summer blue: Quai des Saules, Pont du Rhône, Pont de l'Isle, Quai des Bergues—the Lake of Geneva, wide-shored and open. Sails; the Jardin Anglais, full of tidy people on the benches; and there, the Jet d'Eau, slenderest fountain shaft, white comet of water, self-flung into the sky.

Hôtel Métropole, well kept in gilt and awnings; wide crossings intricately marked, elaborate signals. Place Bel-Air, rue de la Corraterie. Large-fronted banks, slow passage of lustrous motorcars bearing Egyptian and Bolivian license plates, very wide shop windows displaying the single salmon on his block of ice, the one bolt of silk; fruiterers' windows with liqueur whisky, sherry, satin-ribboned corbeilles of tiered pineapple and grape; windows lettered *couture* with nothing in them except a small cut-glass bottle of Chanel scent; and the discreetly wire-veined windows of L'Horlogerie-Bijouterie.

. . . Fifty steps inland and all is changed. An older, smaller, rooted world. The roofs are lower and the façades more simple; dazzle of lake and mountains is shut off: there are plane trees in the square and a little shade, print shops, flower stalls, cafés; women walk by with bread; the Metropolitan Spa is a quarter in a provincial town.

. . . Up corkscrew streets into the Old Town; St-Pierre's, with the bishop's fine stabling below, a scramble over a hilltop, then drawing level to another change— stillness, lines of patrician streets, municipal buildings with private façades, hints of gardens behind walls. In the yard of what may be the Town Hall a father is explaining in *incroyable* French the workings of a medieval piece of artillery and its neat pile of croquet balls to a small boy.

And so on and up, standing, drifting, pushing on, concentrated and aimless, in the manner of a traveller who has neither duties nor timetable, who wants to take it all in but knows that he will not sleep in the town, whose north is not even the hotel but the railway station. A not unrecent Swiss guidebook read, "As we pause in the Bourg-du-Four to buy ducks' eggs . . ." Ducks' eggs!

And who are those who pause and walk on, not with a picture card or postage stamp but with a live, smooth egg in a fragile pale-green shell? I did not find the shop; perhaps its place in the quiescent, crooked square was taken by the shop of the Chinese merchant, Descendant and Successor, the sign proclaimed, of one L. Tschin-Ta-Ni, Fils Céleste, who set up in this very spot in 1779, and where then under the picture of a Dock Road Chinaman, in a penumbra of canisters and an atmosphere of Sherlock Holmesian *sous-entendu* belied by transparent neatness, I had myself weighed an ounce of Gout des Caravanes by a Swiss tradesman with Mongolian eyes, seized by a strong sense of being present in some double exposure of time.

. . . By noon all movement has ebbed away. It is very hot. Summer quiet in the rue Calvin, in the rue du Puits, in the rue des Granges. . . . Only small chink and clatter from area windows and the smell of melting cheese float-ing from doorways where cats lie already curled. Then down the Promenade la Treille, by the ramparts, into those open spaces, those rural gaps, each with its building in pompous, inflated, ephemeral official stucco.

"*Excusez moi, Madame, c'est bien la Société des Nations?*"

"*Point, Madame. C'est un Musée d'Art.*"

"*Ah, et qu'est-ce qu'il y a dedans?*"

"*Des bureaux.*"

Time up. Brief, broiling journey in the trough of the afternoon. In our roomy carriage the blinds are down; the train only hums; it is dark, hot, static, like a farmhouse parlor, yet one is alive to motion and progress through brilliance without. Rolle, Ouchey, Vevey; the train veers north: one last flash, stabbing bright, of Léman, Mont Blanc, the vineyards, gray stone châteaux, and fat-leafed slopes of the Pays de Vaud. Now the green is lighter, the leaves less lush, the trees less high—sweet pasture country, softly molded, orchards, fir trees, cuckoo-clock houses, village spires: the cows have bells. Picture-book Switzerland.

I looked at it with reserve.

HUNDINGEN—WÜHTWILL—OBERWANGEN. . . The light is softer now. Another long valley. And now we cross a bridge. It is the Aar. Look—how snug, how horse-shoe-fitted in its river loop, lies the city of Berne, how small, how held! We stop and I walk into a handmade, child-sized dream.

. . . No. This person in armor and pink gloves on the fountain is a *bear*. And here, on another, is a belted lion in azure, gold-laced boots, and his cloak piped with scarlet, sword in paw, lifting a trusting muzzle to the plumed Good Duke, and on this emerald-and-crimson pillar sits a man in splendid wooden clothes playing bagpipes to a goose, and everything is spouting water and geraniums, and the clock faces are painted too and as large as cartwheels, and there are doves and hares and princes to strike out the hours, and *everything* is picked out in gold and scarlet, and there are thick-blooming flower pots everywhere, in all the windows, and the streets *are* arcades, all the streets, as far as eye can see and foot does carry, and here is a whole square spread with fruit, far into the evening—nectarines, apricots, melons, and wild berries—and everybody strolls or sits or is selling honey-cake or scout knives, and everybody is friendly to everybody, and what they speak sounds so extravagantly homely that it dwindles to harmless absurdity, and nothing, nowhere, is ugly or big or grubby or chic or new.

Then another fast Swiss train streaked towards Lucerne in a long twilight. Next day, early, I took a paddle steamer down the lake to a small resort.

LAKE LUCERNE, AUGUST 5TH ... Midtrunk on the pollarded chestnut trees in the garden by the lake where the schoolmaster and the comfortable lady on the dais are playing Grieg on an upright and a fiddle, and the summer guests and villagers are sitting under leaves and sky in an after-dinner haze while the waitresses stagger by with *Kirsch* and beer, and the lake is rippling and the night is clear, the music earnest and hypnotic and the little colored bulbs glow mildly like strings of insect beads and time is gliding and enjoyment placid and diffuse, midtrunk on the bark, below the buoyant crowns, is a circle of bright metal clothes hooks. From them dangle mackintoshes, leather jackets, summer wraps. And in this garden of middle age and innocence the eye strays to this Swiss skeleton as disturbed as by the supplicants outside the sunny palace in the plaza.

At midnight, when the coats are gone from their indigenous racks and the violin has been bedded in its well-worn case, we examine the trees. It is all right! The hooks are held by an invisible leather brace. The inside of the leather is padded. The bark is not even bruised. We look at each other—how ingenious, how useful, how harmless, how neat. And how housewifely. Like those French crockery shops that call themselves *à l'Agréable et Utile*. But, but . . . "You know, I don't know what to think of that," says Mr. Smith. Nor, really, do I. Mr. Smith was a hotel acquaintance.

. . . The staff are always smiling. "With pleasure." "*Zum Wohl.*" "*Volontiers.*" "*Subito!*" "*Gern.*" "At once." "Please?" "No, thank you—*le service est compris.*" "*Bitte.* Thank you. *Grazie. Merci.* Please." Why?

We had spoken first outside the carved Kodak and news shop, waiting for the boat with the papers to come in, but their names I only learned later on from the register. Mr. Smith *mit Gemahlin und Tochter.* I don't know how they like this, but that's the way it is. The entry plainly conveys what it means—Mr. Smith with women-folk. Herr Camenzind, the manager, strolls through the lounge in a black coat, silk tie, and polished boots. Everybody calls him Monsieur le Directeur. His glasses have a thin gold rim, and he has well-kept hands. His wife wears an apron, and her identity among the service daughters behind the cake and coffee counter is not generally revealed. Herr Camenzind imparts facts, figures, and opinions to the Belgian businessman across the room. The very information I am anxious to acquire. Wages—enough to live on? Well, *yes.* Electrification—pretty general . . . on the farms, for housework . . . For

working people? Everybody works . . . Oh, factory workers? Yes, naturally . . . Yes, nice homes . . . A few very
large fortunes, not many . . . At Geneva mostly, and
Zurich . . . Why, invest it . . . At home? Yes. Hospitals,
museums . . . Taxes? Pay them? Certainly . . . The old?
The old have had time to put something by. . . . There's
things you can do in summer, and others you do in winter. . . . My neighbor now, the one who has the Crown
Inn, he's clerk of Weights and Measures, and secretary to
the council—of course that's not paid—and he works at
a sawmill. . . . You can't sit in a chair all the time. Oh,
I'm an *hotelier de métier.* . . . Unemployment? We have
to have people in from outside each year to help with the
unskilled jobs. . . . Start work early? No . . . the boys
have to get their training for what they want to be; one's
got to think of the future. *All* the boys? On the whole
. . . Find a job waiting? Why, yes—that's what they're
learning for.

Yes. Not really a rich country . . . much of the land
unproductive, got to import food, not many raw materials
. . . Exports—precision instruments: very well; but who
needs precision instruments ad infinitum? or can always
afford chocolate and cheese? We *have* our problems.

"Not being alone on the planet."

Army at nineteen . . . training every year . . . for life
. . . During the war there wasn't an hour when everything
wasn't ready for blowing up the roads and tunnels and
half the country with them. Beggared us? Changed our
lives for twenty, thirty, fifty years.

"You have had the devil's own luck," said the Belgian.

"Yes—luck. With the passes up we shouldn't have been much use to anybody wanting to get through; pity you and the French and the Dutch weren't so well placed."

But to me Herr Camenzind only says, "Yes, it's a fine day. Yes, in winter it's not so fine. Colder, yes. Yes, the war. Hard, yes." Of course the women do not vote in the Confederation.* Everybody seems just as pleased.

———

. . . HOPSCOTCH ON THE paddle steamers—those paddle steamers so like tall mock swans, so white and high, so slow, so calm, so majestic: so crowded—across and back and aslant the lake to the places one might have, but did not, stay at. There are thirty-six village resorts, not counting Queen Victoria's Brunnen (which is almost a town), on Lac Quatre-Cantons, the Vierwaldstaet-tersee, the Lake of Lucerne. All are variations of one pattern. Landing stage and promenade on the shore; the one stone building, the Big Hotel, nineteenth-century, heavily verandahed, well to the front, flanked by confectioners, kiosks, and a spruce little post office flying the Swiss flag on a square of lawn; behind the gabled inns, Gasthaus zur Krone, zum Schwert, zum Schwan, and the Pension Beaurivage; the village street and two general stores with soup advertisements in the windows, more confectioners, a beef and sausage butcher's tiled and chromiumed like a bath in *Vogue,* a cobbler, a master harness maker and two ironmongers, a dairy and a seamstress's sign; a lane, an

---

*They do now.

opening and the wooden whitewashed church with pitched roof and bulbous tower behind the graveyard; then up and out, past the great propped plum tree, over the footbridge and the stream, at once alone, up through meadows, through the stile, up through noon and sudden shade, up into sharper sun and finer air, up the gently rising mountainside.

When I had walked once, I walked every day. Three hours, five, nine. It was like a new grace. Coming out of the hotel in the morning with five francs in my pocket and a stick and starting up a slope, or seeing a boat bound downlake and catching that and beginning from another valley. I could walk over the pass and down to Immensee and bathe in the Lake of Zug. . . . I could get to Schwyz across the Scheidegg and back again through the fields. . . . This was no mountaineering: I never went anywhere I could not lose myself, bumbling along absentmindedly on rope-soled shoes. What did one take? Nature in Switzerland is not extreme, not in summer, not below six thousand feet; the freedom here is freedom also from the pioneer's domestic cares. There's many a discreet amenity—a hut, a shelter on the summit, an inn—where one could eat and sleep and have one's ankle set. A jersey then, and a torch, a knife, and a light satchel to hold them and some food: dry, compact clean food only, hard black bread, hard cheese, and a long, hard, black smoked sausage, smooth like a thin cigar, and for pleasure an aluminum flask to fill en route with spring water and wine. Paper and pencil. An apple one could count on finding on the way. I never took a book.

I met few people except those whose business it was to be about—haymakers in the distance: they were cutting the third hay, a short crop but thick and sweet with herbs and clover; men working the pulleys of a milk lift on an upper slope—but I was seldom out of sight of a cow. The cows of the Four Cantons are fawn-colored, not large, with short horns and unalarmed dark eyes set beautifully in the creamy markings of their faces, and they potter about all day long *où le coeur leur en dise,* eating good grass, leading the best of cows' lives. To keep them from falling over the precipices, the Swiss with unflinching practicalness apply the sensible corrective touch to nature by stringing wires with a feeble electric charge across panorama and promontory. I often lost my way. Once I got soaked in a storm, went on, and came to a house where they lent me a clean, dry garment to sit in. The countryside as usual had been empty, but like Alice's pool the parlor filled at once with dripping people and their boots and dogs. The windows were shut tight against the rain, and there we waited in a smell of wet leather, plum brandy, and soup. When it cleared, the front door flung open, the men looked up on the threshold and stamped their feet before going out, there were shouts of *Adieu* and *Vergelts Gott,* and, before my things had come back from the oven, they were all absorbed again into the landscape. Once it was night before I reached a town; a fast electric train took me to the junction on the lake; there the last boat had gone, but I found that I could hire without fuss a well-oiled bicycle at the station.

The weather of this long, quiescent summer had set at last in full and rare perfection. The granted, still hot days were of a luminous blueness so light and fine, so present, that oneself moving in it felt melted into slow vitrescence. And sometimes from a height one was confronted by yet another blueness—a glimpse of bay below, a rock-set hyaline circlet, suspended lapis lazuli and air, flashing upward light as though a fabled grotto had opened to the sky. Sometimes woods and silence occluded sparkle and the droning noon; sometimes all was space and form. Once I walked all day along a curving ridge that followed but seemed to design the outline of an open plain. Once I ate my lunch in a brook.

What was this magic? The beginning each day the same: the cold, slow, sluggish start with unthawed limbs and disjointed casting mind; the first hour the longest; the first stretch of climb a dull effort. Then came a warming, a change of rhythm, a switch to another strength, and one was in—swinging along at ease, fused in body and motion and mind, in the air, in the sun, the grass, breathing the green and brooks and hay, swinging in the sound of scythe and water, swinging along alone, happiness welling in the heart, happiness made known in a flight of unspoken words, walking, swinging, in a long moment of infinite content.

Par les soirs bleus d'été j'irai dans les sentiers,
Picoté par les blés, fouler l'herbe menue:
Rêveur, j'en sentirai la fraîcheur à mes pieds.
Je laisserai le vent baigner ma tête nue.

Je ne parlerai pas, je ne penserai rien:
Mais l'amour infini me montera dans l'âme,
Et j'irai loin, bien loin, comme un bohémien,
Par la Nature,—heureux comme avec une femme.

—Arthur Rimbaud

Then came some breaks but they maintained the mood.

. . . Zurich for the day. How nice the trains are, how clean. Such pleasure to lean out of the window, got down by twirling a light handle, and watch them put the milk and crates into the van. All done so neatly, on such a man-sized scale. Sometimes the guard takes off his coat and gives a hand. And all *smooth*, never breathless or wasteful: no waiting. I walked down the Bahnhofstrasse in midday heat under trees and awnings—a solid mile of Good Shops. Zurich is the largest town in Switzerland, and one cannot say that this street is not urban—plate glass, streams of people, traffic, stoniest Haussman fronts, and very ugly. Yet there is also a sense of spaciousness and enjoyed prosperity, and nobody looks quite pressed, and it is such a fine day; the trees give shade, and the awnings look bright and cool; besides, nineteenth-century ugliness has lost much of its power these days. The things in the shops make one wish to set up house. This coffee machine will work; this paint job is going to last; this toolbox looks too good to miss. And now the street has come to an end—we stand on a quay by a bridge over a widening river before another lake alive with a hundred small white sails, rowboats bobbing for hire, and beyond the shores and streets and dwindling villas rises a hillside of orchards and, above, a double range of mountains ending, blue and white once more, in snow and sky, and again it is intense, clear, open summer, fanned by a little wind.

And there are two rivers running through the town, and that means waterfronts and water gear, uneven houses with cellar shops and protruding upper storeys, steps and alleys. And across the Limat is a cobbled and timbered quarter, odds and lengths of streets, and squares leading any which way, and old wine rooms with the date painted carefully over the door. I ate shavings of dried smoked beef and drank wine in a shuttered wainscoted taproom with a Swiss family tucking into a large noiseless lunch, a place where one could hear the flies buzz. And then off and all over the town, in the heat, over bridges, checked in squares, chasing the best thermos flask there ever was from glittering sports shop to sports shop, now stopping to look at the new flats going up, now for a distrustful look at the milk bar, now in and out of Zwingli's very late Gothic Minster, chilled and halted by finding it as Protestant churches always surprise me by being so *filled* with varnished pews; now standing to read the playbill: Shakespeare, Anouilh, Schiller, Shaw; now in a bookshop, now in another, picking up a pocket Montaigne—such good print—for half a franc; then finding the Kunsthaus and in it, shockingly hung on a staircase in bad light, a long-sought Claude Monet, the *Déjeuner dans le Bois,* also other treasures: the Man with the Umbrella coming down a tunnel of leaves, Apollinaire with his striped cat at his arm done by Douanier Rousseau, and two or three of those tiny Renoir landscapes . . . Fuselis by the yard and walls of Picasso, and Expressionist Germans, powerful, twisted stuff, composed in an ugly mood; no Klee; what else? but time is up, they're closing. "*So* late," the woman at the entrance had said: "I'm going to mark your ticket so that you can come again tomorrow without paying." I shall not be here tomorrow but did not like to say so; now going out I looked at her again and thought of how much of this there must have been behind the Impressionists, and how little of it behind contemporary painting. And how splendid of the Swiss, how Voltairean, to collect and show it all.

Who goes to these galleries? Who subscribes to the repertory and opera, and hires the sailboats and buys the cooking stoves and good shoes? The inhabitants of Zurich, of course. About a million of them now. And they work in factories and offices, use transport, and live in residential suburbs on the lakeshore. For Zurich *is* a modern industrial town. But how mitigated! The factories do not smoke. There are no slums. Nothing is really far. The town offers something of the scope of urban pleasures of London, Paris, and New York, with less effort, less unbalance, and without the cost in health and nerves. In Zurich, one is aware of the lake at every point, and the mountains can surely be seen from almost any window. It is not an ideal place, but it is still a good one, and in it no man or woman need live, no child grow up, outside the bounds of nature.

Then I went and sat in the Café Odéon, that old haven of Zurich where in cool dimness on worn leather in an atmosphere at once philistine and literary one can read the newspapers of six countries and sit browsing all day over a cup of coffee, and I thought of first causes and of wisdom and accident and planning, of the mess and the lateness, luck and folly, and with sadness of England and with impatience of America, and of the irrevocable duty of casting always, always, the bread of humanism upon the waters.

. . . Into Lucerne to hear Mozart played in the open air at night across a small, cold pond. It was pitch dark, and music and musicians came curiously distorted over the intervening water. The strings, now muted, now carried, floated thin; conductor and violins were reflected, enormously agitated, tail-coated cardboard frogs, head downward on the wavering surface. Was there an echo? The whole quite unreal; lovely, though perhaps too charged with romanticism. Mozart does not need this setting. Emerged trancelike and was glad to find, at eleven o'clock, the friendly animation of the town. Sat by the river and drank some wine, and watched the city swans.

Returned on the boat next morning and found a new ease among the old guard. "*Ça sent la fin de saison*," said the headwaiter. Herr Camenzind is in the wine room with the padre and a bright industrialist from Lille. I am now admitted to these colloquies, at least as a listener.

"We *are* our government," says Herr Camenzind.

The country is small enough, he says—four and a half million—to be a graspable community. The cantons and the boroughs are largely autonomous and run by the inhabitants; pretty nearly everybody knows what he's voting and how it's going to be carried out and by whom. As to the federal government, any measure, on thirty thousand signatures, is put to the general question.

"On paper?"

No, says Herr Camenzind, there's a referendum every other week; and explains also the initiative, a provision by which a man, any man, with the proper number of signatures can propose a bill to the assembly.

"Guillaume Tell."

Not at all, says Herr Camenzind. A recent amendment. 1874.

"What's your president like?"

"Padre . . . ?" says Herr Camenzind.

"On the tip of my tongue," says the padre.

"Don't you know his name?" says the Frenchman.

"He's just been changed."

"Ah."

"He is every year."

"God help you," says the Frenchman.

"Not elections," says the padre. "Council members take turns. Isn't that right?"

"That's right," says Herr Camenzind.

⁓

. . . ASCENSION DAY. Off to Einsiedeln with great expectations. One will never see Dresden or Bamberg now; two weeks ago I hadn't as much as heard of this Baroque Swiss Abbey. It was fabulous.

First the ride in brilliant weather in the open car; over the ridge down to the Lauenburger See, up a mild pass and then through a light forest swiftly into another valley;

the spires, slender gold, visible a long time in the sky and vanishing again as we draw level with a compact, animated eighteenth-century town; a long high street, winding, no issue in sight, then sudden embouchure: a vast square, flown with banners, waters playing, thronged, aloud with bands, and here it lies, the Abbey, wholly glorious in the sun, the sweep of it, in weathered stone, arcades and statuary, the wonderfully rounded center swelling forward as though to meet the eye; one floats across, is wafted up the steps, borne towards the entrance, and now, in a press of people, clergy and a cardinal from Rome, through clouds of incense, one is assailed by flying form, by gold, by white, by scarlet, by wings and swirls and intersecting cupolas and linking angels, felled in one stroke of wonder by prodigy and harmony and daring, swept by the ecstasy, the joy, the beauty—the jubilant innocence of the interior.

WHEN, AT THE END of a month, my meteoric and impatient friend Martha Gellhorn arrived for three days ("I could make it four") from Yugoslavia on her way to London, Israel, and Rome, I was, as well as pleased, dismayed. I did not want to be prized from my lair of discovered joys. I wished indeed to share my store with Martha, but would she see it so? Martha, in a heroic mood, a thousand miles' forced drive straight from Ragusa, with the bronze of an untouched and beautiful country and a people brave as lions still upon her? Martha, who would as soon burn her boats as look at them two times? She seldom has to; and I need not have feared. Twenty-five minutes after she and her small, neatly loaded motorcar had crossed the border, she had seized all. "My dear," she said on the telephone (Martha rings up across countries), "but how clean, how cheap, how honest; how innocent, how comical, how *kind! Why* didn't we come to live here?"

"M.," said I, "I have been up the Rigi."

"Good," said Martha. "I want to see all these mountains; I want to see everything. Can we get to St. Gall and the Engadine and to Bale, and do you think the Grisons? Can we be off at eight tomorrow? Have you been to many doctors? This *is* the place. And we must do all the passes, I did the Bernina and the Splügen this morning, I love them; and I want to see the Rhône glacier."

"I went on foot."

"*Listen*: Where *is* Gersau? Kraut-Swiss, isn't it? Never mind—be with you at five. Lay on a room. I must get some sleep, and perhaps I'd better eat, I forget when I ate last. I want to gorge on all those delectable *Schübblis* and *Pasties* and *Wienerlis* . . . "

"*Zwischenverpflegung.*"

"What's that?"

"In-between-meals taking-care-of."

"Oh, darling—*bliss!*"

She got there, and in the morning we were off on a swift, light journey . . . Lucerne before the shops opened. . . .

"A lake in every town," said Martha. "I do call that stylish."

"It is rather a geological specialty of these parts."

"Any sights?"

"We'll walk around and get them by osmosis."

"I didn't know medieval could be *white*washed. A brilliant idea. Why is one told Lucerne is pompous?"

"Not this part."

"And look at those children's fountains!"

"Wait," said I, "till you see Berne."

"Now, that's the kind of luggage I like, unpretentious, sensible. We must get everything we possess repaired."

"One can send one's bags through the post office."

"Oh, look. Look . . ." Across the road two wax young ladies, one dressed in white tulle, one in pink, were obliging in a store window on an Erard grand. The music open on the stand was a Wolf song; a fire glowed in the grate. On a settee, two suitably gowned matrons and a gentleman in a dinner jacket were listening with gestures of fixed rapture. An old lady had folded her hands over the sewing in her lap, and the master of this apartment had dropped his newspapers. The pink tulle was 87.50. "How much is that in dollars?" said Martha. "You know, I believe one could marry their decorators." She turned to the shop assistant. "I'm sure these are going to be the most divinely comfortable things I ever stepped in, but you wouldn't have a pair that doesn't *show* it quite so much?"

"Madame wishes walking shoes or social shoes?" said the assistant.

"Walking, I suppose," said Martha. "But perhaps looking just a tiny bit social?"

"Perhaps Madame is thinking of a street shoe?"

"Oh, I could hug them," said Martha. "Now I must look for a long time at these watches; we can't afford not to buy everything we see. Now, *why* aren't we exhausted?"

"We have it all to ourselves," I said.

Streamers, strung from thatch to gable, read:

MOTORISTS, PLEASE STOP YOUR
CARS OR DRIVE AROUND.

LEAVE THE INNER TOWN TO THE
ENJOYMENT OF THE PEDESTRIANS.

"Of *course*," said Martha. "Space."

We had elevenses at the Bellevue & Balances on the strip of terrace by the river, flush with the water, where it is almost still and widens towards the lake; and we fed the swans.

"Grand Canal."

"Better," said Martha.

"Now, now," I said.

"Let's shove," said Martha.

We shoved. Along the Alpnacher See to Sarnen; to Sachseln, to Giswel, to Meiringen, up the Handegg, and down into Brigue; to Visp, to Sierre, to Sion, to Martigny, past Aigle, past Chillon, through Montreux, through Vevey, through Lausanne, to Yverdon, to Neuchâtel, to

Murten, to Fribourg, to Berne; we shoved over the Brünig
and the Grimsel, into the South, along the Rhône,
through the Valais, struck west into the Vaudois skirting
Léman and up into the Jura and the borders of France; we
shoved through the Gruyère Valley and the Bernese Ober-
land—*Glissez, mortels, n'appuyez pas*—through floating
space and grim altitudes and mild pasture country,
through cicada country and bare-baked hills, through
lanes and orchards, through woods scented by stacks of
fresh-sawed logs, and through fields one would have liked
to cover with a hand; we saw pine-dark rock never
touched by sun and blanched terraced slopes, gray stone
and tawny stone and honey-colored walls; we saw barns
and chalets, scrubbed village baroque and storybook castles and the elegant lines of residential Louis-Seize, and at
the foot of the Simplon we saw sprung an ochre Italianate
arch. We saw college towns and watch-making towns and
market towns spruce as a new-groomed cat; we saw
shrines at crossroads and villagers on their ways, children
toddling with their satchels, and cattle; we saw funerals
and pulled in for the yellow motor-post sounding a hunting horn; we saw barrels carted to the vintage and the
changing shapes of the straw-stacks; we saw the water
coming down the mountains and saw it run icicle-sharp
through the hollowed tree trunks by the wayside and
spout from pretty basins in the squares; we saw lakes open
as the sky, and we saw the Lake of Thun with its curved
Elysian shore rich with fig and vine. And always friendly,
always light: our progress abetted, smiled at, waved on.

When we were hungry, we ate; when we were tired, we slept; when we were in doubt, we asked. There was always wine, room, a word.

"Can this be twentieth-century travel?" said Martha.

At Sarnen we fell for a manor with chevroned shutters painted white and crimson. "*This* is the place," said Martha. "So pretty, so soothing; and think how one would work. Though what about *l'heure bleue?*"

"There's always a retired major with a collection of Monteverdi records," said I.

"Would he *talk?*" said Martha.

At Sachseln we looked at Brother Klaus, the Hermit Saint of Unterwalden, embalmed in silver armor in the parish church, and wandered about the graveyard among rows of crosses of generations of Zinsalpers and Geishofers. *Hier ruht in Gott* . . . "It must have been so bad for them," said Martha.

"Not incest," said I. "Feudalism. Same seigneur."

On the Brünig we talked ourselves up eight thousand feet—"Do remind me sometime that I'm driving," said Martha—over a road rising gently through soft woods, and when we stopped on midpass, it was winter. We ate ham, trout, rye bread, and apples in a pitch-pine inn with a boiling stove and drank two kinds of white wine and spread our maps and books and spelled out the proverbs on the walls. Then the pass meant business—a stark, unending road climbing, turn above looping turn, into an eminence and yet another eminence of sheer stone, stone on top of one, stone at arm's reach, stone rising; a vastness of stone stretching to gray horizons: and there we were, adhering to the bends with a kind of insane precision, swishing about the edges of the world inside a mechanical mouse.

"So good for one," said Martha. "You know; for the spirit."

"I'm not Emily Brontë," said I.

Martha blew out her nostrils. "I love the mountains."

"A nice hill," said I. "With two cypresses."

"This makes art look small."

"I like it small," said I. "And please may this stop."

It went on. Space expanded; stone rose beyond sea of stone; the serpentine road unwound nine lives. "I admit it is getting rather uncozy," said Martha.

"I am quaking."

"It does make one quake," said Martha, delighted.

And then we saw the hotel on top. Not a refuge, not a hostel, a hotel-sized hotel. "God bless their hopeful hearts," said Martha. "Whom do you think they had in mind for this pleasure dome?"

"You and King Lear," said I.

———

DOWN IN BRIGUE the air was mild. Petrol station and lavatory were clean enough but not *sparkling*.

"Not up to standard," said Martha. "Cisalpine." And then we walked under the arcades of a most civilized palazzo.

At Sion we pulled up as they were saying compline in the darkening church, and sat for a while under the vaulting, the vestments gleaming in the fading light, the voices rising from the choir stalls. *Orate pro nobis* . . . This Romanesque church of Sion is beautiful, and so is the setting of the town in the vineyards and austere hills of the Valais, "the rainless apricot country between Sion and Sierre"; and the town too has beauty, perhaps magic, but it is also—what?—a shade desolate? transitional? run thin? Crummy, Martha said, but no—strayed rather, of two climates, astride like the Rhône towns above Orange, disturbing with intimations. We drank Fendant de Sion, the live pale-green wine of the country, and that night I walked alone in the vineyards above the town and the ruined tower under a cloud-chased moon, stumbling and transported, grazed by twig and leaves, holding the grapes, crushing the berries sulfurous sweet into my mouth. And in the morning we slid off, glad to be gone, glad to be moving, into the scrub and polish and simplicity of Swiss Switzerland.

At Bex crouched a castle large and innocent with turrets and chromatic tiles. A small, long-faced, spectacled little boy informed us gravely in singsong Swiss how to get to the Château.

"Safe again," said Martha.

At noon Lake Léman and the Dents du Midi blazed before us.

"*Can* this be Chillon?" said Martha. "It's become so small."

At Lausanne we remembered nothing. A town, packed and ungelled: brick dust, gaps, new buildings. I asked for the Hôtel Gibbon. But the Hôtel Gibbon is no more.

"*Vous avez toujours le Lord Byron près de la gare.*"

"French Swiss isn't the answer either," said Martha.

But at Yverdon the sun lay on the square like butter; at Morat we saw another manor with striped armorial blinds; and Neuchâtel was all clean provincial handsomeness, long-warmed walls, purring in afternoon calm. We picked up some fruit and washed it in a fountain and sat by another, and ate and talked and strolled and looked into people's windows and wrote postcards.

"What a genius they have," said Martha, "for the small change of freedom."

At Payerne something dropped out of the engine of the car; the man said it would be mended by a quarter to five, and it was.

"Why does it all feel like a balloon outing, when it's really so solid?" said Martha.

"The happy ground crew."

AND ON THE third day, in the morning, we got to Berne.

"I believe in it now," I said.

And there it was, in the sun; a general market spread through the arcades; and there was the black, gloved Bear and there was the golden Lion, "Look at his dagger," "Look at his spurs," and water in all the fountains and flowers in all the windows (may life be like this), and there, rock-crystal green, swirling and seething, straight and wide, was the Aar, dashing itself through the town in an extravagance of foam and speed, and whisked past in it with their laughter the heads of bathing men and boys and women.

"Shall we . . . ? Can we . . . ? Shall we . . . ?"

We have just flung ourselves into the Aar. Four times. Such
a glow. First I did not think I'd have the nerve, then did,
then again, four times. Now we are laughing all over—sitting on the grass in the sun in wet bathing suits in the
people's Free Bath. Chestnuts and lime trees, clerks and
typists in their luncheon hour, soldiers and girls and elderly people, a living *Grande Jatte,* playing draughts, playing ball, reading, eating hard-boiled eggs and sandwiches
from the marquee, drinking things through a straw, rest-
ing from their glory. . . . It is a happy way of bathing, the
most exhilarating I know. First one strolls up the tow-
path, two hundred yards, three hundred, half a mile—in
the middle of the capital, at noon—then comes the long
moment of almost blind decision, then the incredible icy
suck and churn and stunned immediate action when one
must strike at once from the hurling waters of the bank
and gain the smooth-flowing, sunny center, then the
rapid, breath-snatching downstream whirl in the clear,
racing water redolent of moss and snow and mountain
mirth, flashed past shore, roofs, willows towards an alpine
outline, and then it's time—the sluice approaches—to
strike hard once more towards the bank and grasp a passing rail . . . one's missed the second, the third is whisking
by, and here's another: the last . . . feet thrash, knees
graze, an arm shoots out—safe.

  "Again?"
  "Again."

PORTRAIT SKETCH
OF A COUNTRY

Denmark 1962

⌁THEY SAT DOWN at our table, this gentle couple, after a shy smile of inquiry. He wore a stiff, dark suit made of good stout cloth, a waistcoat, and a clean shirt with a low, round collar. There was a wedding ring on his stout, slow, well-scrubbed hands. She was a small woman, thin, just not frail, and she wore a white blouse trimmed with embroideries under a jacket of old-fashioned cut. On her hands, which were small and finely shaped, she wore a pair of transparent gloves made of some light lace, and these she did not take off, not even when she came to eat, morsel by morsel on the little fork, the slice of cake brought to her on the pretty china plate. They were country people, country-bred, and they had come to enjoy the wonders of this pleasure garden and the world. They were both utterly brushed and festive, but the most remarkable, the unforgettable thing about them was her face.

His face was placid and honest, the face of an honest fellow, with that look one finds in the North, in any North, on hardworking people of good stock, on peasants, on sailors, and also on laboring and contented beasts. Her face was goodness incarnate. We all have become used to the ease with which we can convey nastiness and horror; their opposites have no such ready currencies. I can only try to put down what in fact I saw. This woman's face, then, shone with pure, sheer, golden goodness, with gentleness and innocence and patience and a kind of grave alertness; it was an open face, water-clear, and one could watch the movement of the slow, good thoughts across it. *She*—stout fellow though he was—was worth ten of him.

You knew that he might well be a bit of a fool over the mortgage, a bit of a brute when in drink or with the ox and plough, but she was there, she was always there to make it right. They scarcely spoke; she did not bustle or fuss or pour out his coffee; she just sat with him, but you knew that she was looking after him all the time. They were not holding hands, but they sat as if they were; they sat in still awe, seeing what had charmed their parents and *their* parents and *their* parents for a hundred and twenty years now, and what we, too, saw for the first time—the old, tall trees under the night sky with their summer leaves made emerald young again by caverns and splashes of light, by Chinese lanterns glowing fat like tropical fruit, by luminous dragonflies large as sea gulls, by quicksilver shafts of water; they saw the fountains, the pleasure boats floating upon the artificial lakes, the ducks and live swans;

they saw the Pagoda, the pavilions, the toy soldiers' parade, the high swing of a trapeze; they heard, muffled, shrill, inviting from across water, from beyond trees, the strain of fiddles, the rise of fairground voices, the swish, the cracks, the sudden cry, the laughter; the drumbeat, clangs and crashes from booths and roundabouts and Russian railway, the call to the fireworks, the pantomime.

At last our couple rose. In her gloved hand she held the bill for their refreshment. She read it once, they read it twice; her lips formed a figure, his repeated it: their eyes met in wonder. She took out a purse and, incredulous but happy, they arranged a little pile of silver.

―――――

WRITERS (OF GENIUS) take some traits of their people as they find them and blow them up; the people take in that larger and explicit image of themselves and grow to live up to it. This process may go on for a good long time, through generations, but it does not last forever. Fewer Spaniards look or act today like Don Quixote; the Balzacian strain appears to be weakening among the younger French; very little (un-self-conscious) Dickens is left in contemporary England. Daisy Miller is seen no more, and Babbitt himself is far from what he used to be. In the 1960s a good part of the people, the houses, the habits, and the look of things in Denmark are still pure Hans Christian Andersen.

Andersen was a man well on in his thirties when the Tivoli Gardens opened in Copenhagen in 1843, twenty acres of trees, lawn, and lake in the center of the now largely modern town. This enclosure is still intact. The illusionist's summer-night world has changed little—the same décors (beautifully repainted), the same props and shapes, the same commedia dell'arte; serene and unrowdy, the crowds mill and partake, the young and old, the simple, the civilized; but let there be no misunderstanding: if there is naïveté in the pleasures offered at Tivoli, there is no artlessness; there is a sound, almost fundamentalist kind of showmanship and some uncommon technical skill—the fireworks are superb, the swings fly fast and high, the rifles at the ranges shoot loud and true, the slot machines spit (and swallow) hard live money, and the standard of the variety shows is as good as the best in the Americas and Europe. And as for the pretty little confections of anchovy and leaf and jelly and shrimp on creamy whorl, served in pretty colored cups and dishes on a dozen flowered terraces by pretty ladies, these are not so much meat and drink as gracious living substantiated, gracious living not out of the magazine but out of the fairy tale.

This delicate and somewhat dreamlike nightlife flourishes among a people otherwise solid, stolid salt and earth, a nation essentially of farmers, craftsmen, seamen: but then even the Andersen tales themselves are not all snow and thimbles but robust with such facts of Danish daily life as acres, horse troughs, straw, and winter fuel. It must seem that the good Danes have some particular talent for getting the best out of the basic and the complicated, the old ways and the up-to-date, the land and the machines. And a talent, also, for continuity, that so disregarded human need, a talent for tempering and humanizing change. The castle, the church tower, the manor house, the cottages, barns and yards and fields look as if they had stood here, been tilled that way, for a hundred and another hundred years. Beside the porcelain stove, the beams, the inherited tables and chairs, the sleek herd and the mare nursing her foal, you will find harvesters, electric ranges, separators, churns, the latest devices of agricultural and domestic know-how. The people on these farms are (mildly) prosperous. They read. Fifteen books, in fact, if you go to the statistics, per head for every one book in the United States, but a great many books less than in Finland, where the nights are even longer and the electricity is cheap. They eat much and well, veal and cream and butter and buttermilk, fresh and smoked pork, smoked and fresh fish, slabs of great round dairy cheeses, potatoes, eggs, pickled beets, and sound black bread. The Danes work hard—but not backbreakingly hard; the work is not ill rewarded or degrading; it is work of care, and those who do it belong to the land, and the land (or 95 percent of it) belongs to them.

Indeed, half the Danes live in or off the country. "Half the Danes" means two and a quarter million (they are, luckily for them, not overpopulated—yet); of the rest, one-quarter are compressed in Copenhagen; the others live in small towns. Dapper small towns with market squares and waterfronts and flowers in the casements, arcades, patrician houses, and a folk museum, every one of them prettier than the other and no two of them quite alike. Of course the country itself is a small country, how small one only realizes on learning that it is in fact the size of half of Scotland; a Scotland, at that, fragmented into one chunk of peninsula (Jutland), one fair-sized and two smaller islands, and some five hundred tiny islands, one hundred of them inhabited. From any point of Denmark no one is ever out of easy reach of the sea: a beach, a jetty, a ferry, or a sailing boat. And these thousand coastlines, these bays, these rings of sea are complemented by inner circles of still water, marshy lakes flat-set into the land, and village ponds under the willow trees, round as a hole, round as the cartwheel that props the stork's nest on the thatched rooftop.

The weather changes with the sea winds, and the winds change twice a day. The overall climate is cool, gray, blustery, rain-sprayed, a climate that may just do for winter, autumn, spring, but cannot quite make summer, at least not every year. The Danes, with their worship of the sun and their joy in outdoor pleasures, do not have the climate they deserve. Yet who knows, if they had been reared in some tropical latitude, by some warmer shore, they might perhaps not have attained that very deservingness. And when it *is* fine in Denmark, when for an evening or some morning hours the sky is clear with that light Nordic blue, asail with cumulus clouds white as a ship, as swift as down, the fineness has a gossamer quality, an essence of calm and rareness. It is the weather of childhood, some ideal childhood fixed in an Impressionist vision of spade and bucket on beach and the long grass of the dunes.

The Danish countryside, too, exercises a soothing charm. Tilled to the nines, not quite flat, uncluttered— there is always a long view to the horizon—green, flaxen and red with pasture, ripe barley, cornflower, sunflower, and poppy, the scene of centuries of man and nature going hand in hand, it fills the eye and mind with measured calm and peace.

To get about, on wheels, afloat, on foot, is unfrustrating, easy. The ferry steamers and the fast, clean electric trains run like clockwork and running ply the willing travellers with food, *snaps*, and beer. Stationary sustenance is provided on terra firma by country inns that go by the engaging name of *Kro*. The roads and side roads are good and, apart from the six-lane Copenhagen-Esbjerg highway that crosses the country (and the seas), innocent of traffic. Copenhagen is another matter. There, the traffic is not only dense but (Denmark is not without its psychological riddles) ruthlessly fast, as fast as the most headlong Italian driving though without the Italian dash and driving skill. This death race is intricately regimented by a spider's network of white lines and guiding lights quite sensibly worked out, provided you live long enough to learn the ropes.

The learning must be voluntary; there are very few traffic police about, or indeed any visible police at all. In three weeks of Copenhagen we never saw a policeman on patrol by either day or night, and as capitals go Copenhagen is well on the noctambulistic side. Anyone who so wishes may drink in a public place all night; sensibly and tolerantly, the government does not interfere; when one bar or café has to close, there will be another about to open, quite legally, down the block. Likewise, it is always possible in Copenhagen to find someplace to eat hot food around the clock, respectably and at the normal price. Incidentally, it is *Sweden* that has all these restrictions on the buying and consumption of drink; it is Sweden that has the alcohol problem. And Denmark is *not* the Scandinavian country with that high suicide rate. Denmark is a part of Scandinavia; so is Canada a part of America. Danes, Swedes, Finns, and Norwegians are Scandinavians in the way that Americans and English are Anglo-Saxons and Brazilians and Bolivians are South Americans. Denmark once owned Norway and ruled Sweden. Norwegians up to a hundred years ago spoke Danish. Now Denmark and Norway and Sweden are neighbors, and good neighbors. They share some of their outlook and their policies. There are affinities. Looked at from the outside, and even from the inside, they have a good deal in common, and a good deal that they have not. Readers may recall Miss Katherine Anne Porter's Swede, Arne Hansen, in *Ship of Fools*. Herr Hansen, admittedly a knotty character, flies off the handle when persons he is introduced to take him for a Dane and when corrected wave aside the difference. Swedes are not Danes, and Danes are not Swedes and not Norwegians, and they would have you know it.

———

ONE OF THE UNIQUE things about Denmark, and one that it is not easy to convey, is that this rural, this bourgeois, this deeply democratic country without class handicaps, without great fortunes, without poor, this solid welfare state where a social-democratic party has been in office with few interruptions for about forty years, not only possesses an aristocracy and lives with it harmoniously but has itself in many ways an aristocratic air. Look at the architecture. The very cottages have line and grace, and those small-scale seventeenth- and eighteenth-century manor houses (inhabited) that are everywhere have an elegance, a fantasy, a style to them, that takes one's breath away: they are ravishing. They are also unexpected—dazzling white picked out with slate gray, they are entirely unlike anything one could meet elsewhere in those temperate parts, in Holland, Austria, or Germany; if there is any reminiscent link it is, oddly enough, with the domestic baroque of Northern Portugal, those delicious nunneries and *quintas* of the Beira and the Minho. Perhaps not so oddly, the Portuguese like the Danes were once a seafaring, predatory, and adventurous nation—and how far, how far apart! have they travelled since.

Architecturally, Denmark also has its ample quota, lovingly preserved, of the more conventional sterner stuff—craggy dragon castles and vast ornate Renaissance boxes spectacularly sited on seaboard or parkland, the homes nowadays often of schools or the old. And then original again, another unique delight, pink-washed medieval village churches, Aslev, Højerup, Morgenstrup—one could almost invent the names—painted inside and exquisite in form.

Architecture without pain, art looked at in undiluted pleasure, enjoyment without anxiety, compunction, heartache: there is no beggar woman in the church door, no ragged child or sore animal in the square. The water is safe and the wallet inside the pocket. There will be no missed plane connection. We are in a country where the curable ills are taken care of. We are in a country where the mechanics of living from transport to domestic heating (alack, poor Britain!) function imaginatively and well; where it goes without saying that the sick are looked after and secure and the young well educated and well trained; where ingenuity is used to heal delinquents and to mitigate at least the physical dependence of old age; where there is work for all and some individual leisure, and men and women have not been entirely alienated yet from their natural environment; where there is care for freedom and where the country as a whole has renounced the drive to power and prestige beyond its borders and where the will to peace is not eroded by doctrine, national self-love, and unmanageable fears; where people are kindly, honest, helpful, sane, reliable, resourceful, and cool-headed; where stranger—shyly—smiles to stranger.

Tak is the word for thank-you, and the Danes thank one another all the time, when they hand or accept an object, when they put fork to food, when they rise from table, when someone has said thank you—*tak, tak tak, mange tak, tak for mad, tak tak*. And caught in that virtuous circle the foreign visitor, too, soon goes about clacking like an amiable turkey cock.

WAR AND THE THREAT of war begin when all is not well at home. Countries that solve their own problems are no problem to others. How did it all come about; how did the Danes get that way? Why are they what they are? Was the country particularly favored? Did they try to keep the peace in the past? Did they practice religious tolerance? The answers are no. Is it then all hit or miss? A people holding a territory poor rather than rich, with a history as long, mixed, and disturbed as the next country's—are these the facts that must be fed into the computer, and what might the computer's answer be? Portugal? Switzerland? Prussia?

The most cursory catalogue of Danish antecedents bristles with the violence, confusion, and vicissitudes commonplace in European histories. The computer would have been told about Viking terrorist raids (the Vikings of course being the forefathers of the Danes), successful invasion of England, the line of rough-hewn kings: Haarik; Harold Blueteeth, who forced his subjects into Christianity and subjugated Norway; Gorm the Old, who had a slogan for his conquests: "Denmark's Repair"; Sven Forkbeard. Been told about expansion in the twelfth century; dynastic disputes; absolute monarchy; a chain of regicides; invasion of Germany; nobles' risings; conquests and reconquests culminating in Valdemar the Great and Danish Ascendancy, hegemony in the Baltic, rule over the whole of Scandinavia, Estonia, Holstein, Greenland, Iceland. Strife; decline; division; Reformation and religious wars; the Bloodbath of Stockholm; the Counts' War; participation, inevitable and debilitating, in the Thirty Years' War. And so it went. By the end of the eighteenth century there was a wind of change, relief from oppressive taxation, improvements in justice, some liberty of the press. By the nineteenth, Denmark's troubles came thick and fast: in 1801 a British fleet (Nelson) bombarded Copenhagen; a few years later the Danish fleet itself was destroyed, Norway and Sweden gone, a rough deal at the Congress of Vienna. Fifty years later, American and Australian influx of cheap wheat was pricing Danish grain out of the European markets, and Bismarck embarked on the first of his planned wars, and won. The Prussians—so much stronger—took Holstein, South Schleswig, and a huge chunk of Danish Denmark, North Schleswig. It was a devastating defeat. Denmark was left nothing but itself: a country the size of less than (at that point) half of Scotland, a country with no metals, no iron, copper, tin, no oil, no coal, no colonies, no overseas possessions (except the Virgin Islands, which only went to the United States in 1916). A devastating, a traumatic defeat, and the Danes might well have fallen into a Treaty of Versailles mentality. Mysteriously, they did not. Instead they redirected their aims and will; they did turn inward. They changed their agriculture from grain to dairy products, they set up cooperatives, gave their attention to social and economic advancement, chose a neutral policy, developed an altogether new kind of adult schooling. It was a chain reaction, but the links gradually forged themselves into a virtuous circuit. It has turned out well.

Why—we are back again at our original question—
were the *Danes* able to use a particular chance, one they
could then hardly have seen as such, in a beneficient way?
Did national character determine their choice, or did the
choice stabilize that character? Perhaps, for want of a better answer, all one can say is that Denmark at one point
entered a phase of historical luck. *Tak*. Long may it last.

NOTES ON A JOURNEY
IN PORTUGAL

1958

PORTUGAL BEGINS AT PORTUGAL. For days we had been progressing across the immense and empty landscapes of Castile and Leon under a driving rain, quaking and shivering inside a small, slow motorcar, a couple of pygmies creeping over the face of the earth. Under that planing sky, the land stretches, treeless, unconcerned, to the far and low horizon; now and then throws up a cluster of flat clay huts. At the Spanish frontier post—adobe to adobe—there was no one on duty; I had to go back some way, still in the rain, to find two soldiers, thin as crows under their black lacquered hats, to stamp our exit; three hundred yards farther along, the Portuguese customs sat squat and mute in a trim white house, sparkling rings on their fingers.

Stares, but no questions; slow, blank scanning, a foretaste of the general Portuguese reluctance to terminate a transaction, to let go of any piece of paperwork; then a flickered half smile, the lifting of a barrier brightly painted

like a lozenge at a fair, and we were in a river valley shining with new leaves—there were magnolia and oleander,
fig and eucalyptus, water chestnut and spring maize,
haystacks pressed like sugar cones hung from the boughs,
and along the roadside the young birch trees were gar-
landed with vines. Lyre-horned oxen, under painted
yokes, advanced hoof before slow hoof; women moved by
with forests on their heads. Against the cork oaks leaned
shepherds stiff in raincoats made of straw. Rococo shrines,
white picked out in gray, stood upon the hillsides, water
gushed from tritons' shells, and at the end of many a
flowering orchard there could be had a glimpse of the
pediment of a small manor house. It was Cimarosa, the
Sette-Cento, a setting to some bucolic masque—we had
entered one of the most innocently beautiful regions of
this earth; we had entered into an Arcadian dream.

It never fails, this first sense of pleasure, light as feathers, of the land entry into Portugal. Whether one comes
into the Minho through Galicia or into the Tras-os-
Montes from Leon, whether one arrives in the East by the
Salamanca road or from Spanish Estremadura in the Alentejo, there is always that entire and abrupt—and never
wholly explicable—passage from the harsh sublimity of
Spain to the slow-moving, lyrical beauty of the well-
ordered, handmade, water-freshened countrysides of
Lusitania. And there is also of course the arrival by sea,
the first look at Lisbon from across the Tagus. One cannot go wrong with one's first step.

Ten minutes later we were in Chaves. Even the rain
had stopped; the sky was gentle blue. (By sheer chance;

it rains, alas, a great deal more in Northern Portugal than in those plains of Spain.) All Portuguese towns are pretty; some are very pretty; a few are exquisite. Chaves is charming and dotty and unexpected. The houses, all the houses, are painted green or pink or blue or tiled, and have delicate balconies, each of some faintly out-landish eighteenth-century shape. The corners of the roofs turn up in a pagoda tilt. There are arcades. Every-thing stands sparkling clean in the light sun. The chief trade appears to be the sale of very large polychromatic trunks. The whole effect is of a pastiche whiff of the Far East with something of the spruceness and well-being of a small town in Switzerland.

On the Spanish side it had been too early for lunch-eon; here it was too late. In actual time it was now a lit-tle after two o'clock. Everything was *fixado,* shut, closed down, fixed—a most favored word. The gaiety and light-ness seem to be confined to nature and to stone and stucco; it is not reflected in the people's clothes or faces. Male peasants wear inky tatters; the men in cafés wear inky business suits; the women are beasts of burden in field and street, and otherwise not seen. We retired into the car to think. Instantly we were surrounded. Por-tuguese stares are blank and black, immovable like flies on butcher's meat. You turn, you whisk, you say something: they are still in front of you. The disturbing thing is that there is no curiosity. The faces do not see. No flicker of interest or communication animates them. Speech effects no breakthrough. Ham, the good smoked mountain ham of the region, is *presunto* (prshoont), bread is *pão* (pong).

The general recipe for pronunciation is to forget every-thing one has ever heard or learnt of Spanish and Italian, to lop off final vowels and as many others as laziness sug-gests, drawl out the remaining ones, change any conso-nant into one easier to say, replace all *s*'s with a double *shsh*, aim at a nasal twang (a blend of Cockney with Meridional French will do), sing the whole like Welsh, explode it to sound like Polish, and do not forget a hint of Dutch. Begin with the name of the capital: *Leeshsh-bowah*. The trouble is that the Portuguese will not even try to listen to your efforts; they don't believe a foreigner to be capable of managing a single sentence. And there they are right, of course. They themselves—outside the Lisbon-Cintra-Estoril circuit and the big hotels—firmly speak Portuguese and Portuguese alone.

A DAWDLING afternoon drive got us to Vila Real. Vila Real has two streets that end by their (baroque) façades joining in an arrowhead—a startling architectural turn, dexterous and graceful, that one finds again in two or three other places. Here we were at a crossroads. A choice had to be made. One could be at Oporto before night-fall—on the threshold of the port wine country, one need only go up the Douro . . . from there perhaps try getting up into the high wild parts, the *serras* of the Tras-os-Montes, to Mirandela, to Vinhais, perhaps reach for far Bragança. . . . There is so much to see, so many places—names—one is drawn to, and what one sees is so fresh, so different, so ravishing, that one wants to linger and enjoy. We did not want to leave the fertile North, the Elysian pastures, the land of light and fanciful, white-trimmed domestic baroque. For days we went about in circles.

We went to Vila Mateus, the most fantastic of eighteenth-century country houses, the like of which could be seen only in Portugal, and in Portugal only once; we went over the Serra do Marão and came down from the heights and out of the pine woods and had luncheon in the sun at Amarante by the river, looking at the tiled cupolas and the bridge with the obelisks; we crossed the Tamego and here, in the province of the Minho, the Arcadian dream thickens, the vines grow higher upon the trees, oranges are ripe, melon and roses flower beside the gentle cornfields, slow the wheel turns by the well—so idyllic is the countryside that, in the words of Sacheverell Sitwell, "the action of passing through it induces a mood akin to that of being in a trance." We went through Guimaraes and saw the colored palaces and streets; we came to Braga with the twenty churches and saw the golden organs, and slept in moonlit quiet and cool—in an excellent hotel—in the sacred garden at the top of another architectural extravagance, the ornamental staircase, pilgrim shrines, and fountains of Bom Jesus.

Vila Verde, Ponte da Barca, Ponte de Lima, charmingly spread along a riverside, Barcelos, Valença, Viana do Castelo—*quintas* and convents, façades bat-winged and sea-scrolled, *manoelino* doorways, *azulejos*, painted ceilings, barley-sugar columns, formal gardens, markets in the squares, octagonal chapels no bigger than a sentry box and crumbling monasteries vast as railway stations, flowers in the ruins and statues in the fields . . .

Everywhere the wine is pleasant and very cheap. I have a fondness for the *vinhos verdes,* the slightly (naturally) fizzy wines of the Minho: the white, which is very dry (*too* acid, sometimes) for apéritif; the red, which is reminiscent of some young undoctored Tuscans, with simple food. I recommend, too, the red wines of Colares and of Dão (Dong) and a crystalline pink wine made at Vila Mateus. If one is looking for vintage port one will be disappointed; what is sold in restaurants and shops is sound enough commercial stuff. Great port is drunk chiefly at the English shippers' and growers' tables, where the hospitality to travelling strangers is Dickensian, Oriental, something no longer met with elsewhere in these diminished days. Food is agreeable, plentiful, fresh, and unaspiring. This goes for the country in general; at Lisbon and Oporto restaurants, the standard is either lower or higher. Olive oil and fish are always excellent, and the bread is often. Beware of large round loaves that look like dark country bread: that is *brua,* maize bread, and as heavy as wet cement. Butcher's shops are best left unvisited by what the French screen warnings call *les personnes sensibles.*

AFTER A STAY in satrap comfort at a port-wine *quinta* and some lonely days in the extreme wilds of the Tras-os-Montes, we found ourselves once more at Vila Real, from where we had started weeks ago, on our way at last to the more known regions, to the lions of the traveller's Portugal. Two-thirds of the country lay still in front of us—the towns of Guarda, three thousand feet in the air; Lamego with its peaches and baroque; the double staircase, chessboard statuary, and nine landings of Nos Senhora dos Remédios fantastically covering a whole hillside; Viseu incomparably elegant; Oporto; Coimbra with its undergraduates in black tailcoats at noon and the magnificent library; Obidos, alas much manhandled and restored; Evora classical within medieval walls shimmering in the heat of the Alentejo; Estremoz and Elvas, the white towns of Estremadura, brilliant with Arab domes; the unique abbeys: Alcobaça, a Cistercian shell; the lovely *manoelino* fantasies of Batalha and the stupendous Convent of Christ at Tomar; São Jéronimos at Lisbon, the Tagus, the Alfama quarter, Black Horse Square, the golden coaches and the tower of Bélem; the dank woods and hermitages of Cintra so dear to our forebears; the gardens and pink palace of Queluz, a Lusitanian Trianon; the sea—never far!—the white fishing ports with their curious craft, their glaring cubic huts and smells of tunny and sardine: Nazaré (self-conscious now and tourist-proud); Setúbal; Sesimbra; Olhão in the Algarve . . .

MAIN ROADS are not bad and, except for some busloads of pilgrims, unencumbered. Side roads can be frightful. Native driving is individual; like Edwardian chickens, the species has not yet bred the survival qualities required by a motorized society. Good hotels are very good; not-so-good ones, tolerable; the rest are either what are called *dormidas* (mixed dormitories and no drains) and quite unbelievable, or do not exist. The *pousadas,* the government inns, often set on a cliff or a hairpin bend at the dizzy edge of some panoramic wilderness, are near perfection of comfort, quiet, and general pleasantness. They are exquisitely clean and not at all expensive. One can eat and drink and take one's time in Portugal without having to think much about money. Bills are honest, easy to read, and without those vexing taxes and surcharges that one finds so often in Italy and always in Spain. Hotel room prices are posted on the bedroom doors, and stuck to. Bargaining, even if one could attain to it, is blessedly unnecessary, although that is not what one's Anglo-Portuguese friends will tell one. According to them, their beautifully arranged domestic lives—five servants is a modest minimum—are spent in a perpetual robbers' den, a view that seems to be shared by the Portuguese well-to-do, judging from the way they keep themselves and their goods under lock and key: at nightfall the countryside resounds with the bolting of shutters and the barring of gates. One may assume that they are spoilt and no longer aware of the contemporary world and its ways. During a long stay—complete with housekeeping, servant coping (*one* servant), car repairs—we found the Portuguese people, who work very hard and very long for abominably little, touchingly honest. The modern Portuguese are in fact a mystery. Travellers have complained about them bitterly for centuries—ruffians, robbers, brawlers, filthy, lazy. Now they are browsing, placid, kindly, patient, slow. Laundry is being washed morning, noon, and night; a second-class hotel or a Lisbon boardinghouse is ten times cleaner than its equivalent in France or England. There is no quarrelling in the streets, hardly any crimes of violence in towns or country. Bullfights take place in an atmosphere of a garden fête that takes rather long to get going, and nobody is ever killed or hurt. Aside from the inveterate staring, they are kind to strangers and take endless trouble. If you ask in a shop for something that isn't there, half the staff and all the customers will walk out with you and down the street to find you what you want. This does not succeed because when a Portuguese accompanies a foreigner he automatically becomes a foreigner too in the ears of his compatriots, and they can no longer hear him.

Foreigner: "Tmat'sh?"
Portuguese shopkeeper: "Euhhh—?"
Portuguese accompanying foreigner: "Tmat'sh?"
Portuguese shopkeeper: "Euhhh—?"
Second Portuguese accompanying foreigner: "Tmat'sh?"
Portuguese shopkeeper: "Euhhh—?"
Portuguese child accompanying foreigner seizes some tomatoes from a basket.

After this they all flock out again and into the next shop to find another item. Painstaking, patient, kind, placid, slow. Above all, very, very, very slow.

A JOURNEY IN
YUGOSLAVIA

1965

First Hours

⟿ NEW GROUND, these days, is rare. On this clear May morning we have left Trieste, that sparkling, opulent, friendly, noisy Western port; the glittering sea road winds steeply towards the Yugoslavian border. I am driving slowly: pleasure, curiosity, are tinged with apprehension—I am about to cross into a socialist federal republic, into what must be, however mitigatedly or loosely, a curtained country. A string of Italian cars warily pulls up behind me, and I feel obliged to put on speed. Travellers' tales about the roads had made me decide to keep my own car at home and to rely instead on a huskier, and expendable, hired one. When the rented Fiat was delivered in Florence I had been disconcerted to find that it was snowy white, like the proverbial sacrificial lamb, and appeared to be, though fast and willing enough, a rather nervous creature. As we set out on the Via de' Tornabuoni, intent on getting on the right bridge for the *autostrada,* I became aware that other cars were keeping a quite unusual distance. Not one tried to cut us off at corners; not one raced us to the traffic lights; we were given precedence at every turn. This puzzling circumspection, so contrary to the nature of Italian motorists, continued on the open road. If I waved a driver on, he would hang back. We stopped to get some lunch at a gas station—broiled chopped steak, spring vegetables, iced pink wine, chilled apricots, black espresso coffee—one of those new mass roadside eateries that the genius of the country (it *is* no less than that) had endowed through the sheer cleanliness of the surroundings and the brilliant freshness of the food with a character of exquisite luxury. It was here that I gave another sharp look at the alien Fiat; so did an attendant. "You *are*," he said, "from Naples?" And before I could say oh-dear-me-no, I tumbled to the mark of Cain or talisman that had bewitched our journey. It was the letters NA on the registration plates. NA for Napoli. For some good reason of their own, no doubt, the firm of car-lenders had seen fit to provide their hireling with this dashing identity. Neapolitans on the road are dreaded for their skilled fiendishness and nerve; theirs, in a land of pretty nippy drivers, is a reputation for lawless daredevilry. So here with the NA large and clear for all to see was a Neapolitan car, manned what's more by that improbability—legend also has Neopolitan wives and daughters harem-bound at home—that superlative of terrors, a Neapolitan woman driver. Handsome is who handsome does. Reckless is who reckless seems. Inevitably, I tried to live up, at moments, to my suggested second driving nature.

And now we have passed Fernetti, the Italian frontier post, a wave-on—as has now become the good European custom—rather than a full stop. *Buon giorno, buon viaggio.* A few hundred yards of no-man's-land. Another barrier, new flags: a sweep of stripes, blue/white/red and the Red Star large in the center. Fernetti has become Fernetic. We stop. I switch off the engine. I repeat to myself the words of the official handout (*all* handouts in a state-controlled economy are official; the government as it were underwrites the ads), "The customs procedure for foreign travellers when entering or leaving Yugoslavia has been reduced to a minimum." I step out, a light, fixed smile upon my face. An official approaches. Our passports are looked at, seriously. (Car papers, not at all. Liability insurance, rather alarmingly, is not compulsory.)

"What have you to declare?"

I open the boot. The man peers but does not touch; he seems reluctant to take initiative, reluctant to let go. He is not surly; he is not friendly; he is hesitant and intent. Intent not to slip up. And at once I am on familiar ground. This might be Portugal, Central America. . . . It might indeed be the vanished Habsburg Empire on whose physical ground we are standing. It is a sad, perennial pattern: the more overweening, the more unchecked the top, the more rigid and at sea the lower echelons, the undereducated, underpaid, under*trusted* functionaries of the sacrosanct bureaucracy. These anxious, stubborn men are held to cleave to the letter, and the letter here is transparently double-faced. Smooth passage for the tourists; inflexibility about sections 214 to 315(b). I decide to help by declaring my typewriter. At once there is grist to the mill. I am told to enter an office; here other men of the same stamp—stamped by the same conditions—are at their task. Forms are made out.

"Number of the machine?"

"I don't know that it has one," I answer and am aware that this is not the right tone. The men do not insist. Their task is extrapersonal; they have not been encouraged to show either arrogance or servility (which might perhaps have come more naturally to them, for something of the Habsburg administration must still be in their bones). I sign. My passport is endorsed. There is no duty to pay. The sole object of the exercise is to keep me from selling the wretched instrument during my stay in the country or from giving it away. If I should lose it (unlikely) or it gets stolen (unlikely too, one hopes), I might find myself in hot water. Presently it's all over; I am back in the car. The barrier is raised. It has not taken long after all. The handout's first promise was honored. Our journey has begun: we are off. We are in. We are free.

The road is wooded, less wide; motor traffic has dwindled, and there is a peaceful trail of horse-drawn carts. The names on milestones and posts read Škocjan, Tržiè, Kranj, Vrhnika, though the alphabet up here in the North has not changed. The leaves on the trees are the same early-summer green, and in the distant blue we still see the delicate outlines of the Julian Alps. Deliberately, we dawdle. At the crossroads a beflagged booth proclaims itself a MJENJAÈNICA—WECHSELSTUBE—CAMBIO—BUREAU

DE CHANGE. I return from this moneychanger's with my notecase stuffed with dirty dinar notes.

"How pleasant it is to have money, heigh-ho!" It is noon by now, and the day is perfect. Our aim is Ljubljana: a town of a hundred and fifty thousand, the capital of the state of Slovenia. In a new country I find it not a bad plan to begin in a place of middle size and save the coasts and the great sights, time willing, for later. But now it is too early and too fine, and the town is already near. We decide to outflank it, to turn north, to follow the valley of the Sava and drive towards those mountains. The result is some hours of blissful drifting through a prealpine land-scape. And before sunset we reach a lake. It is Bled, ringed by massed Alps light as cloud, light as blancmange, though close now, snow-topped, slate-blue and white: below a still, dark water cradled in the setting of a Cen-tral European children's tale. Tall, dark trees descend to the shore; the craggy castle perches on the backdrop cliff; there is a tufted island, jumping fish; small rowboats jog their moorings. Happily we walk along the lakefront, spinning flat pebbles upon the glass-green surface.

Ljubljana

At dusk the outskirts are packed with trudging people, pedal bicycles, cars; the buildings are aflutter with long banners, the national colors, the state colors, the red party flag. Workers trekking home? a general holiday? Ignorance makes stupid. At last we draw up on Tito Avenue near the hotel. These, we had learnt, are government-graded from A to D; there are at present about thirty A hotels in the country, and Ljubljana has two of them. We chose the older one, the Slon, the Hotel Elephant. Once more best smile forward, I enter the lobby, which is packed, and make my way to the reception desk. A friendly young man assures me in good English that a room—with bath—is to be had. We have to hand in our passports before a key is surrendered, though mercifully are not required to do any paperwork ourselves. When I mention luggage, the young man says that just now he is over-whelmed (which is visibly true) but will try to give us a hand when he can. We start to cope on our own, and the hard part is not the weight of suitcases but the density of people through which they have to be wedged. Unavoid-ably we brush against other belongings, bump into sides and legs. Nobody pays attention: they do not appear to see or feel. Presently our receptionist, assistant manager, hall porter turns up to help, and the emphasis *is* on help, on helping out, not service. The institution of the bellhop appears to be unknown.

At last we are in; alone in that traveller's daily goal, the hotel bedroom. The door is shut. I turn taps, switch lights, open wardrobes—everything is reasonably clean, functions reasonably well (one cold tap trickles, one sheet is mended); there is decent if slightly shabby comfort. In most Western countries the hotel would pass muster as good B minus.

Almost at once I go out again into the streets, intent on immersing myself in the stream of evening life. The shops are about to close, but food can still be bought, and drink, and the coffeehouses are alight and the bookstands. It *is* a national holiday, a day celebrating liberation, but it was also a working day: there are lava tides of people both receding homewards and seeping in, sluggish and determined, a dark, compact mass oozing over the pavements, stagnating at corners, filling up the squares. Their overall aspect is one of sallowness, burdens, and poor clothes—raincoats and exiguous suits in muddy colors, mustard, gritty gray, off-brown. It is the all pervading drabness of one's image of the streets of Moscow, and it is this congelation of people—to be encountered over and over again—that blots out all other first impressions. It is not a crowd as we know it, a crowd of occasions, New Year's Eve, Trafalgar Square, a crowd in elation or panic; it is the incidental crowd of a permanent rush hour—too many people in too little space—cohesive only in a material sense, composed of particles obtuse to one another, struggling towards single ends. Immersed in it, I experience a sensation of hopelessness.

———

DINNER AT THE HOTEL RESTAURANT: a cozy Germanic cellar, soon rent, alas, by loud, thumpy music. Piano and one violin, live. No hat is taken round; the musicians, like the cook, are state-employed. One of the waiters speaks some German, another a little Italian; neither is enough to interpret the dishes. Never mind. I had taken care to provide myself with some thirty words of Serbo-Croat (Srpskohrvatski), things like *Good morning* and *Please* and *How much* and *Thank you.* I had also rooted out and put to memory a pocket-sized gastronomic vocabulary, the names for meat, shellfish, vegetables, how to say *iced, hot, grilled, boiled.* It is no great feat, and yet those Slav nouns, however cavalierly you leave out the inflections, are not household words. *Maslac* does not trundle off the tongue as easily as *burro* does for butter, nor *odrezak govede* as glibly as *bifteck* for beefsteak. Now, hunting through a complete menu, I was getting baffled, practice as so often making a hash out of theory; with a busy waiter at my elbow and the cutlery quivering with a gypsy waltz, I could not quite identify a single word. At length the sauce-stained polyglot menu was produced. I have never found these to be very accurate or literate, but here some bold if unspeculative mind had solved the problem of translating (into five languages) with neat consistency. Krumpira Soup—Soope de Krumpira—Zuppa di Krumpira—Krumpir Suppe, this accomplished document began and went on to tempt the customer with Cutlets Serbian Style, à la Serbe, alla Serba, nach Serbischer, Art, Bosnia Style, Slovenia Style, Istria Style, and so on with blithe economy down the list. Knowing I had lost that round, I ordered one Bosnian and one Dalmatian style. What came—after a goodish wait—were large platefuls of meat and very little else, one of them undoubtedly pork, the other a miscellany under pepper and tomato sauce. Quietly we swallowed the lot: we shall never know which had been which.

(Only days later, having left Slovenia, did I realize that Federated Yugoslavia is in fact still multilingual. The dice on that first evening had been loaded against me: in the manner of someone trying Italian in a Mexican restaurant, I had been pitting rudimentary Serbo-Croat against good Slovenian.)

Later on at night the crowd on the pavements has thinned, though it is still a crowd, and the cafés are jammed. There are young people about—this is a university town—girls on their own in groups or pairs, looking purposeful and animated. The boys sport jeans (large KO-BOJS stitched across back pockets) and have fine sulky eyes; they look virile and glum, handsome in a lean, dark way. The middle-aged look less Slav and more Central European, soft-hipped men and square-built women, with here and there a painfully worn, thin one, and the few old people in that crowd look a different breed again. They are peasants of another age, groping along the pavements, strangers strayed into the city on some errand.

Our night walk leads to the river. We stand on a bridge. Here there is peace, old houses reflected in still water, and the glamour night bestows even on quite modest architecture.

MORNING CONFIRMS that Ljubljana is a pretty town at heart. That corner where the river curves *is* charming; there are some passable baroque buildings, an exuberant fountain with an obelisk, a few pink- or apricot-washed façades. There is also the castle, a Franciscan church, a subtropical garden, and an opera house—much in use—left from the Habsburg days. Add to these flowerboxes in windows and a view of Alps—Ljubljana may well appeal to those who are fond of Austria, except that those might prefer to take their Austria neat. Pretty at heart, but the heart of the capital of Slovenia is a shrunken core in a shoddy contemporary spread. It is what is left of an old town on a strategic crossroads that has undergone its share of history. What Augustus founded, Attila razed. After Romans and barbarians, Slavs, Austrians, Napoleonic armies, and Austrians back again. Each pulled down, each built—1919 brought national independence, 1941 Nazi Germany, 1945 independence once more, this time with a communist regime. And under those auspices the 1950s and '60s brought the Modern Age in its most graceless form.

Only the Turks, who for so long occupied the other parts of present Yugoslavia, never took Slovenia. It does not bear the scars of what are called the Turkish Centuries. Hence today the consciously emancipated, the Occidental air of Ljubljana, where the women study mathematics and girls are allowed out alone at night in public places.

En Route

We have left behind the mountain valleys of Slovenia and are progressing through a wide, rich plain. Young wheat, tobacco, corn, fruit trees. We are bound for Zagreb on the Sava (on the principle that one ought to spend a few days in at least one of the big cities). Zagreb is the second largest, only some hundred thousand below Belgrade, and reported to be the show window of the republic, abundantly stocked with consumer goods and *Kultur*. The road is the central highway that runs southward through the country from Austria to Greece. The eighty-five miles between Ljubljana and Zagreb are officially classed as a motorway. In fact, it is a wide road, barred to animal-drawn vehicles, accommodating, but not divided into, four lanes and without separation from oncoming traffic. The surface, for miles on end, is excellent. A pretty fair effort one might say for a country whose technical and financial resources are not exactly unlimited. If it were not for the potholes. These appear at irregular intervals deep and sudden on this declaredly fast road. Sometimes there is a warning sign, as often there is not. You can feel in your spine what would happen if the car slammed into a hole at seventy-five an hour; what one does is to skirt the hole by a wild last-second swerve, praying that the devil will not get the hindmost.

Fortunately, the traffic is on the thin side. The proportion of foreign tourists' cars is very high. Cars run by Yugoslavs are either very large or very small, polished Mercedes—often bearing the red number plate denoting a high official—or tin cans.

We have made two stops. I must mention them because they pointed up what I would learn to recognize as the two main themes that confront the traveller in Yugoslavia, themes that run parallel at times and often intertwine—the country's great natural and architectural inheritance and its present way of life. The first stop was at the snack bar at a filling station. We picked our way through a barrage of trucks and light motorcycles. Inside it was packed with men. The air was hot and smelled of cigarette smoke, stale clothes, spilled beer, and sour milk. The floor was thick with stubs, food parings, and other waste products; the counters were wet and cluttered with smudged glasses and used plates. Behind them a man and youth in stained overalls valiantly strove to cope. They were not speeded on by their equipment. Soft cheese had to be balanced on a pair of copper scales against a set of fiddly little weights; the thumb that had handled the dinar notes was pressed into the Spam-type sausage while the other hand was busy with the slicing knife. The customers ate and drank. What mattered—one felt—was their being able to earn enough to do just that.

The other stop was off the road on the green banks of the river Krka. There was an idyllic little island tethered by a wooden bridge, and on the island an old manor house in a shady scented garden, turned into a hotel. Roses were in flower; there was quietness; waterfowl swam past. It was, in fact, enchanting—as restful and pretty a half hour as anyone would like to remember on his travels. By the roadside there were waiting some official and some foreign cars.

Zagreb

The center of this city, which was once under the Hungarian wing of the Dual Monarchy, is all vast squares, wide avenues of heavy gray buildings lined with dusty trees, and rectangular public parks filled with troops of shirted youths being led off to some meeting or excursion; something of the Balkan climate, of harsh winters and steaming summer rains, appears to have seeped into the paving stones. The Palace Hotel is a not-very-cheerful relic—plush and gilt need keeping up—of pre-1914 splendors. The main staircase seems to have been narrowed, though there are still palms on the landings; the rooms are still high-ceilinged, the beds vast, the tubs deep, but the tasselled cord no longer pulls the faded curtains, the casings of quilt and pillow are coarse and patched, and in the bath there is a smell of drains. (Let me add that there is an alternative grade-A hotel in Zagreb, a brand-new leviathan by the railway station with car park, air-conditioned cells, and Western service.) From the billboard in our lobby one can see that there is plenty going on. A soirée of folk dancing, a symphony concert, a repertory opera program, an exhibition of contemporary sculpture, and the play tomorrow is going to be *Who Is Afraid of Virginij Vulf?*

At the post office (the hotel porter, not untypically these days, knows the postage required for a letter to the United States but not to England, and at any rate his stock seems to have run out of stamps of any useful denomination) there are long queues in front of every window. I spend a salutary twenty minutes standing in one of them. Salutary, because it seldom comes amiss to experience at first hand how the other half lives. The postmistresses look learned and are certainly efficient and quick. The snail's pace is caused by the quantity of their clients, who for the most part do not look as if they corresponded often or with ease or were accustomed to tying up cash in anything but the instantly consumable, and by the minute volume of their business—one man, one letter, one stamp.

Yet education is one of the regime's most proclaimed concerns, and in the cities one does see many well-lit and invitingly arranged bookshops. There is apparently a large market for translated fiction. The bulk of it is classics: English, French, American. Contemporary writers such as Sartre and the existentialists, who were illegal a few years ago, are now admissible, but publishing houses and faculties are still hampered by very limited allowances of foreign currency to pay for translation rights. So you may find an entire showcase devoted not to *Peyton Place* or *Naked Lunch* but to Džek London and Mark Tven (*Tom Sojer*), easily spotted under their light Serbo-Croat disguise, and, rather harder to unmask, Džejn Ostin and Fenimor Kuper (*Postdnje Mohikanac* by the latter is a clue).

The shops are full. Of goods and people. The goods are of poor quality, and there is little or no choice, everything being allotted from some state manufactory or canning plant. Prices are high; that is, a shoddy pair of shoes costs about as much as a good pair in the West, and, as people earn a great deal less, the real cost, say, of an overcoat or an electric stove would seem to be quite shocking.

We found a touch of opulence in the sight of men at breakfast in the boulevard cafés. They start off with a jigger of slivovitz, that tough plum brandy, and light a Turkish cigarette—everybody smokes like chimneys—then appear coffee, smoked ham, and eggs. The eggs come bubbling in a little copper pan, hot, irresistible, and freshly made. We took to them and found that North or South, town, village, or resort, grade A or C, this was the dish that never failed.

We went for a Sunday walk up the hill into the old quarter of Zagreb. There are churches, vistas, traces of fine buildings, and row on row of low houses in various stages of decay: peeling plaster, damp patches, broken shutters, paintless casements. . . . These human habitations bear the signs of overcrowding, dirt, discouragement, a state of being where the purchase of a pot of paint is beyond moral and material means. A man's spare suit is hanging from a nail on an outside wall. In a doorway a woman with bespattered ankles, bare feet in slippers, is beating her small boy with a switch; the boy has been handling his toy football clumsily. The quarter is as picturesque—under a gray sky—as the back streets of Naples have been said to be, and it turns one's stomach.

Farther down a cookshop sells for a few coins a creamy-crusty concoction of macaroni and white cheese hot off the stove, called *burek*. There are no tables, only a shelf that runs shoulder-high along bare walls. A young man comes in, not ill favored in appearance; he takes his plate of *burek*, puts it on the shelf, and, head down, hands dangling, begins to eat with his mouth, face in plate. One can see that he is entirely practiced. When his plate is clean, he leaves the shop. Not a word was spoken, not a glance exchanged.

We walk back, down into the official town, along the avenues drained by Sunday quiet. All is empty, remote and still as if one had sunk beneath the surface of life into a vast, gray crater.

The Sixteen Lakes of Plitvice

Sixteen Lakes—a range of lakes flowing, tumbling, cascading one into the other—and a hundred and one waterfalls! It was by luck and the word of a friend that we went there. The guidebooks' synthetic gush is sprayed impartially upon the mediocre and the sublime. It might have been a public show of one of nature's larger stunts, an hour of shepherded gaping with one's fellow sheep; it is, the waterplay at Plitvice, an enchantment, a scene of solitude, of infinite and slow and varied wonder.

All went well from the beginning. A few hours' drive; an excellent road—the lakes are enclosed in a national park in a mountainous region of dense forests; arrival towards evening; the sound of water, the first breath of the deep, cold, tree-fed air. The ample hotel is on the edge of the park; the snug, spruce, well-designed rooms smell of fresh-cut pine. Dinner. Sleep. Breakfast, some easy clothes, a map, a ticket, and one is through the gate, left free, all day if one so desires, to stroll mile after mile through a water-landscape that is at once primeval and still changing, a glorious and fantastic configuration created by century on century of interaction of water, stone, and vegetation. The upper lakes are broad and placid, deep-shored, set among old trees, maple, flowering ash, hornbeam, mountain elm; the middle lakes are swifter flowing and of many shapes; and on the lowest levels they are compressed to frothy, turbulent inlets that have cut themselves—with what tremendous force—into a narrow canyon. Everywhere is plant life—shrubs, wild flowers, rare mosses, ferns, on the banks, under water, on the rock face, subtropical, alpine, hydrophilous; but the dominant, the all-pervading, element is water, live water in every phase—water on the move, on the roll, foaming, whirling, swishing water, rapid water toppling over cliffs in suicidal dash, still water, majestic water, horizons of water, tinkling water splashing in elegant quicksilver rays, hissing water spouting from stone and earth, thunderous vertical water roaring skyward in strong jets, folds of creamy water descending in soft cascades.

There are pools, there are brooks, there are streams; grottoes and caves abound. There are miniature, Chinese-sized water gardens; in one clearing stands a perfect semi-circle: here the falls have reproduced in water the architectural shape of a Greek theater. And as one wanders immersed in the profusion, now stunned by roar and speed, now becalmed beside some peaceful pond, captivated by yet another flourish of light and leaf and spray, one is walking also through a landscape that is a natural prototype, one that the masters of the baroque never did see but must have dreamt, and to the wonder of which they gave shape, less innocently, on another scale, in the fountains and façades of Rome; so that here, in the limestone mountain ranges of deepest Croatia, one can recall the related raptures of Trevi, Quattro-Fontane, and Navona.

We allowed ourselves to stay three days.

The Dalmatian Coast:
Rijeka—Zadar—Šibenik—Trogir—Split

Back to earth, down to earth; not unpleasantly so in this easygoing, not unprosperous seaport. There is often a tinge of civic freedom to be found in large shipping towns, whatever the color of the dictatorship. Rijeka, moreover, once known as Fiume (remember d'Annunzio and his private capture of the port in defiance of President Wilson and the Allied Powers?), belonged to Italy as late as 1948, and something irrepressible seems to have remained. The crowds in the drab clothes are here, but they look less Slav, less monolithic; they are crowds that stand and stare *all'italiano*. There are plenty of ships in the harbor, a brisk smell of salt and sea, good-looking food in the markets; the town hall is ochre-washed and gay with a huge round clock face; the small pink churches in the back alleys are charming; and the price of the standard cigarettes changes from street to street.

Rijeka is a starting point. It is here that the classic traveller's route down the Dalmatian coast begins; here that the tourists—in the new skyscraper hotel with the view over weathered roofs and sea—sort out themselves and their baggage before taking ship for Dubrovnik or a dozen islands, or the road south as far as it will lead.

We took the road. A few miles of shrubby trees and suddenly one is out under the sun and hard, dazzling mountains, bone-bare, bone-white crags, jagged, piled high into the sky; and on the other side the quiet blue sea, view upon view of smooth, deep bays and islands, always islands, stretching low in a slight mist tawny and light as the bloom on a peach. All day we drove, drenched in that beauty. At noon we ate ham, fruit, and bread on a promontory; a peasant woman clothed in black lay full length under three blades of shade; the mountains shimmered, the sea below was glassy still. At sunset we reached the Zadar peninsula. The most wonderful drive, we said, we had ever experienced.

There are things to be seen in Zadar, the ex-capital of Dalmatia—Roman gates, ramparts, an early Christian church—but the town is spread out thin, without a defined center, and so rather invertebrate, and I found it drab again, deprived and sad with that whiff of sleeping-underdog melancholy to be found in poor places ruled autocratically. For the transient, however, there is easy escape: a couple of miles out of town to the beach and pine woods of Borik, to an agreeable hotel in a garden giving straight onto the sea, with good food and clean, uncomfortable rooms. While we were there the jasmine was in flower, and the garden at night was filled with sweet scents and the song of nightingales.

The coast immediately below Zadar is tufted green with small, rounded, bosky mountains; farther south it becomes fertile with figs, olives, vines. Less astonishing than the blanched mountainscape of the day before, it is still beautiful. All at once the road ends. Ends. There has been no forewarning (except fine print on the map). We are at the edge of a wide bay among a phalanx of impatient cars. There is no choice now except to take a ferry; to queue, to be precise, for this compulsory service. We wait; we pay up; we grumble. Midway across, we forget: for there is rising before us the sight of an old town of mellow stone, fan-shaped, a hemicycle spread-eagled upon a rock wall high above the sea. The vision grows: it is Šibenik, founded and fortified nine hundred years ago, the veteran of a score of wars between Venetians and Turks, of prosperous, powerful past and placid present. We land: the promise of the approach is not belied; the inside is as lovely as the shell, compact, almost secret— narrow, shaded streets, steep and vaulted, a Venetian piazza, sculptured lions. . . .

It is too early in the day to spend more than a loitering hour; this town is only the first encountered of the string of Adriatic ports of high beauty on this magic coast. Less than thirty miles farther south is unique Trogir, the Tragurion of the Greeks, perhaps the most flawless of them all, a walled town on an island reached by bridge. Here, everything from the rare Croatian-Romanesque basilica in the sun-soaked square to the city gates is harmonious and untouched. Nothing is new, nothing jars.

Another drive—the sea is translucent green now, afloat with small, tortoise-mound islands; the mountain slopes have turned stone again, lavender-gray stone, but cultivated (by what crushing, patient labor) into stone fields, immense ones, of sparse symmetrical vines—and already we are in Split, in Spalatum (I find it hard to use the contemporary Slav diminutive for a place so filled with Roman echo). The first thing one is struck by is the animation: on the quays, in cafés, under awnings, move-

ment is spilling over the pavements; Spalatum is no
museum piece but an active port, a live city alive with its
own business of which the sightseers are only a part; a
city, also, that encloses within vast inner walls another live
city, the nine and a half acres of classical ruins, later jux-
taposed with Romanesque churches and Venetian gothic,
that had once been conceived as the abode of one man,
built for the life and death of the Emperor Diocletian.
That palace and mausoleum were begun in A.D. 295, and
when they were ready, Diocletian—Gaius Aurelius
Valerius—himself a native of Dalmatia, abdicated the
throne of the Roman Empire at the age of only sixty-one
and retired. With him there was housed within the palace
walls a court of attendants, guests, guards, and slaves
amounting to two thousand souls. At the emperor's
death this place of unmanageable size became public
property and was accommodated now as an army camp,
now as a marketplace of refuge from invasions; gradually
the rooms and banqueting halls were broken up and par-
celled into private dwelling places, new architecture was
piled on old, Christian churches were raised on pagan
ground. Nowadays, as one enters this core, this inner city,
in the evening, as one should, at the hour of blue dusk,
one finds oneself inside a hive of slit streets and small
piazzas, alight with bars and stalls, bee-loud with chatter,
clotted with milling people. The Venetian façades have
delicately arched windows and twining balconies trailing
vines; all is a gracious commixture: pillars rise from fountains and birds nest on the pillars, columns are topped by
roofs and the roofs by bushes—it is an easy pleasure to

stroll here. A sudden turn, and one's breath is caught: here under a rectangle of intense night-blue sky, empty and dark, stands a colonnade—we are in the peristyle, the inner temple above Diocletian's tomb, the core within the core. A black sphinx crouches; there are two lions; the place gives off an impression of immense stillness, of imperishable being at the end of the tunnel of time. It is not large, the peristyle in Spalatum, no larger than a casual corner of the Forum: one stands, seized at the throat by emotion, the sense of having come near the heart of classical antiquity.

Adriatic Islands—Dubrovnik

A storm kept us land-bound in Spalatum before we were able to take ship. The least said about these vessels the better. They are not big; they are not very clean at the beginning of a voyage, and at the end they are indescribable. The passengers are packed like sardines, only, as someone said, sardines are neater. Officers, stewards, crew, salaried officials to a man and unsusceptible to tipping, are impervious to the discomfort of their charges. Bands of schoolchildren and adolescents—who may travel free in any class they choose—swarm over saloons and decks. Their comportment would make American children look inhibited. They are oblivious of living human flesh: the floor, a deck chair, the breathing form inside it, are all the same to them, a defense mechanism, we decided, developed by the perpetually overcrowded. If you are four or six to a room and can never be by yourself, you must come to treat your brother and aunt as so much furniture or go crackers. They plump their knapsacks on anyone's knees, dig elbows into elderly bosoms, eject sweets from mouths onto anyone's clothes. A youth sat down on my feet, guitar and all; another propped his tin of tunny fish, open and oil-dripping. on my lap and set to eat, while a girl reclining against my side spat sunflower seeds—all done as un-self-consciously as a dog would crunch a lamb chop on the carpet in the living room. One realizes that here no educational countermeasures are likely to be taken by parents, school, or public press. The parents cannot alter the living conditions; the schools do not incline towards indoctrinating bourgeois manners; gracious-living columns do not (yet) exist in the magazines. What one wonders about is the future. Will it be a graceless, stark new world? or might there be a revival either of humane or formal manners? We may know more when, or if, prosperity at last arrives in Yugoslavia. The islands are worth the journeys: Korcula—birthplace of Marco Polo, a hedgehog-shaped round town encircled by orchards and beaches—Bräe, Hvar, and a hundred small others. The climates are sheltered, the sea marvellous to swim in; there is diving, fishing; birds, wild fowl, endlessly varied vegetation, walled towns; pleasing harbors abound. . . . Like the mainland, the Adriatic archipelago is quite fabulously endowed with scenery and architecture.

Farther south is yet another charming small resort, called Miljet, and still farther—by frightful road—two walled towns, Budva and Sveti Stefan, and above all Kotor, the medieval port at the mouth of a deep-cut bay where cathedral spires rise against the tremendous Montenegrin mountains.

The Istrian Peninsula: Pula—Poreè—Portoroz—Ruminations—Piran—Last Hours

Time was running out. Having begun the journey as we had in Ljubljana, we had missed a stretch of the coast, the Istrian Peninsula, of long Venetian occupation. Perhaps it is a mistake to leave it to the last, to see it spoilt and sated as we were, for it is good travelling country. The roads are never far from the clear sea; one passes alternately lush vegetation, salt flats, charming villages, vineyards, olive groves, oyster bays. The towns look gay, graced as they are with their campanile, with loggias, pilasters, lacy arched windows—oh yes, the Venetians have been that way—and it is always easy to find a good, simple place to eat. For the sightseer there are many casual treasures and there is Pula, a somewhat rusting port, with a pleasing Roman temple and Augustus's amphitheatre staring white, massive, impressive from the outside, rather falling apart within; and there is the very, very fine sixth-century basilica at Poreè with its glowing Byzantine mosaics.

At Portoroz, port of roses, another storm overtook us, the sea went wild, and we spent a day of rain and frustration in the largest hotel's largest room while the wind was shattering the glass in the windowpanes. I lay in a vast sunken bath of very hot sea water, thalasso-therapy, and ruminated on our journey. What had been best? What had been bad? And what else? What else did we see? Where else did we go?

There had been the days, strenuous ones, in the Moslem parts (a million Yugoslavs belong to that faith), the drive through Bosnia-Herzegovina into Serbia to Sarajevo. Herds of goat and pig; women in Turkish trousers of flowered stuff but faded and caked with mud (it rains hard and often in those parts), toiling under burdens by the roadside, in the fields (no studious Portias they, like their Ljubljana sisters); Banja Luka and a first glimpse of mosque and minaret; the Turkish cemeteries, curiously moving, lying abandoned, overgrown with weeds, their gray headstones mounted by sculptured turbans, weather-worn, snail-smooth; the drive through the rocky, gorge-cleft Vrba valley, and the Bosnian fortress town Jaice standing on a cliff above two riverfalls. The monster road, the nonroad, the forty miles of holes and stone and mud that shook every screw and bone and had to be ground through in second and first gear, which made one pray at every jolt and wish that one had hired not a car but a brace of jeeps (one for spare), but to which our white eggshell of a Fiat (which I had been treating with the anxious care one always bestows on the neighbor's child rather than one's own) stood up gallantly. The increasing evidence as one went south of century-encrusted poverty and sloth; the mean, box-shaped houses without a lick of paint; the silent, watchful children; the lean-ribbed cows; the chicken tethered by a string; the scarceness of the petrol pumps; the stop where a sheepdog was so ravenous that he seized and wolfed down a whole loaf of dry bread in one single snatch; the up-to-date hotel where the chambermaids—ageless drudges—went barefoot and the tablecloths, absorbing egg stains, grease stains, soup stains, ash, remained unchanged from breakfast till night; the disarming friendliness of the hard-worked men and women on the solitary roads always mustering a wave, a smile, to salute the stranger splashing comfortably by. Sarajevo of haunting memory, where one finds that a street is named for that earlier Lee Harvey Oswald, Gavrilo Princip, and a plaque put up to mark the spot from which he fired the two pistol shots that murdered the Archduke Ferdinand ("The shots that killed seven million men"); Sarajevo, a teeming hotchpotch of Balkan and Oriental, mosque and business streets, *souks* and slums, and an atmosphere of contrivance, limitations, restlessness—nothing ever, perhaps, quite safe, quite clean, quite straight—that produces its own kind of galvanized vitality but makes me cry for Switzerland. Mostar, still deeper south, more stagnantly Oriental, with the wonderful old Turkish bridge of one great arch.

What else? A sprint into Montenegro, land of incredible mountains and the brave. The hair-raising ascent of Mount Lovcen—by huge touring bus driven with steadfast skill and care by a middle-aged Croatian family man; I have seldom seen such driving—view opening on stupendous view turn after corkscrew turn; noon hours in quiescent Cetinje, the old capital; a visit to the Royal Palace turned museum—an armory, a billiard table, "This was the King's dining room—Do not step on the carpet," cabinets with photographs of mustachioed nineteenth-century gentlemen hung with small arms or stuffed into frock coats bristling with decorations; the somnolent square where males of a recognizably similar stamp slouched aspitting ... And what else? The skull-and-bones scare signs warning against reckless driving, the huge posters depicting green-tinged skeletons gripping the steering wheel as the car hurtles over the precipice in flames. The contrast everywhere between the old architecture of the country and the new, which was nearly always without merit, garish, shoddy, daubed with loud but dismal colors, chocolate brown and magenta being frequent favorites. The megalomania of the official sculpture, the monuments to liberation, industry, and war, so reminiscent of what Mussolini used to perpetrate.

Food. Even in out-of-the-way places you will get a fairly well-cooked meal, sounder and more plentiful than you could expect in similar localities in France or England. There *are* shortages, and the variety is often small. The chief lack is fresh fruit and vegetables. Distribution and preservation are at about the stage they were in the West a hundred years ago: you can get only such vegetables as are in season and are grown nearby, so in winter and some places you get none at all. Yugoslavia goes one further because even if there are broad beans, lamb's lettuce, and cherries on the market stalls, the A and B hotel restaurants will seldom alter their menu of state-canned peas and salads of pickled beet and cabbage. We got by in these by ordering lemon with our tea, chopped onion with grilled meat, and the excellent stewed fruit that is always on. Starches, curiously for such a Middle European–inspired cuisine, are parsimoniously doled out, a few sticks of potatoes, a scooplet of rice, and expensive. A minute helping of limp spaghetti costs as much as a full-sized pork chop. The mainstay *is* meat. Veal and pork, some beef. Steaks are not bad, though below Anglo-Saxon conception. Chicken, when it is to be had, comes grilled and is as good as any I have eaten, if not better. The same goes for fish. Scampi, mullet, fresh tuna, bass, straight out of the sea, hot off the grill, of beautiful flavor and firmness, are served in harbors and side streets.

The cooking blends from the Austrian into the Balkan. Veal on the bone in the north, veal stuck on skewers in the south; but far the best food is to be found in the Italianate parts. Privately owned, family-run pensions and restaurants have recently become allowed. Quality in the grand official places varies. At Plitvice it was fair; at Split outstandingly good. Indeed, in small places inland and in regions of poor supply, the restaurants of A and B hotels are your best bet, whereas on the coast or in the cities I would always rather go to the native grilleries and taverns.

Yogurt is served everywhere, in large jars, and is particularly good. Tea is stained water, coffee a misery. In Slovenia they use espressos and a few real coffee beans; elsewhere it is coffee stretched with roast barley and malt, wretchedly flavorless and thin. There is more body—and coffee—to the sudsy, syrupy Turkish brew that comes in those copper pots, but it isn't everybody's taste, and certainly not for breakfast. One must do as the provident Germans do who carry their own tins of instant.

Wine is cheap and drinkable. I would not put it higher. Cigarettes, Turkish and some Virginia approximations, are very cheap, loosely rolled, not strong, and, I am told, not satisfactory to the heavy smoker. Beer is poor stuff, and everywhere there is slivovitz, that fiery plum brandy, which is quite wholesome and costs only pennies. In the cities and at Dubrovnik are special shops where foreigners paying hard currency may buy Scotch whisky, American cigarettes, and other articles not available to the inhabitants.

Language. In spite of Slovenian and Macedonian, Serbo-Croat is the official language of the country. The few words of it one is able to acquire during a journey will be of some slight help in sorting out Entrance from Exit, Right from Left, Open from Shut, and they will please the Yugoslavs. Unlike other nationals, who prefer to show off a foreign language and will not thank you for massacring their own, they display a childish pride at your uttering two syllables of their speech. For your real needs, you will find some German, Italian, English, or French (in that order of frequency) spoken nearly everywhere. *Spoken,* not necessarily understood. People may talk to you in English with deceptive fluency without really catching on to your answer, or your question. This is never admitted and may cause disappointment and confusion. So do not be too certain that because the nice girl at the desk has said Yes when you asked to have your washing back before the boat on Monday, you will get the washing.

And the Yugoslavs, how do they judge their own condition? Do they feel hopeful? resigned? content? Do they feel trapped? Do they feel free? It is hard to answer. For one thing, their terminology of freedom is not ours. For centuries these people were great fighters for freedom; they fought and they fought—to drive out barbarians, Turks, Venetians, Austrians, Italians, Nazis; they fought each other. What they fought for was an idea of national freedom; they did not fight for *individual* freedom, for *civic* freedom; democracy has never been a living concept in the Balkans. Now that they have driven out the invaders, their intense sense of nationalism is satisfied. One must remember their inheritance of misrule and oppression; also the fact that most of the Slav people who now constitute Yugoslavia were hostile to one another during most of their history. Now they are united; there is internal peace—certainly a desirable and desperately difficult achievement. And the price is Tito Communism. It is not possible for a short-term visitor to say what they may feel to have lost, may feel to have gained; whether, for instance, the lack of the freedom of political choice has any reality for them. *We* know that the Yugoslav regime is far less totalitarian and more Westernized than Moscow Communism (and may become more so), but do the Yugoslavs themselves look at it in terms of East and West? One does hear some criticism—among the highly educated—some skepticism about far-flung economic plans, is told of discontent among the peasantry, who have had the very dirty end of the stick: attempted collectivization but no social security, no health insurance, no old-age pensions. (Yugoslavia is far from being a welfare state, and people will hardly believe what you can tell them about postwar England.) But discontent and criticism appear to be on the fringe of general acceptance and much pride in the state of things: the young know nothing else; the middle-aged remember the war and occupation; some of the old have seen better days, some worse.

As for the foreign tourists, they do have their freedom. They may go where they wish. There are no compulsory guides, no factory tours, no proscribed areas. If you happen to pass what may be a military installation, there will be merely a pictorial sign asking you to keep out and not to take photographs. No one waves a gun. You are not bullied (except when you cross against the light as a pedestrian). You can eat and drink at most hours; wear what you like. The beaches are blessedly unprudish. Unlike Spain, there are few police in evidence. You do not feel, and I think are in fact not, followed or spied upon. This applies to the foreigner going about his holiday, changing his money at the official places. I do not know what might happen if he tried to poke his nose in a bit more. People do talk to foreigners, and some will talk freely, but they lower their voices when doing so and first look over their shoulders.

THE SKY CLEARED that evening in Portoroz. It was our last night. We went out to eat some fish. Next morning we departed. I had left Piran, the most Venetian of the Istrian cities, to the end. As we turned the bay, the whole port came into view, in the clear Adriatic light, the front of painted houses at the edge of the water and their reflections, like a sea mirage, red, umber, rose-pink, and blue; a lovely farewell.

An hour later we were through the border, my typewriter checked out, the dinars turned in: fifteen English shillings' worth, the exact lawful amount. On the Italian side we declared our Turkish cigarettes, two hundred each. "Two hundred packets?" the guard said and grinned. In Trieste I stopped and bought the *Times* and the *Herald Tribune*, the first English newspapers in many weeks. In the hotel I left a stack of letters at the desk to be mailed, ordered and drank a cappuccino, then shot up in the lift. I was happy, very happy to be back, and glad to have been away. One day, if the gods be willing, I shall want to go again, go again for the freshness and the utter change; for the translucent sea, the round towns, the proud architecture; for the mountains, the incomparable scenery; go for the sense of wonder and renewal at the sixteen lakes; go for the islands; go for the sight of Spalatum, Trogir, and Piran.

LA VIE DE CHÂTEAU

A Diary in Bordeaux 1978

⟶ JUNE 1978. Bordeaux Airport at three in the afternoon is quiescent. (A provincial airport, small; we feel human.) The French, who can be so good—and at times so horrid—are putting their good foot forward: affability, intelligence, uptake. The rented car *is* there. Outside, it is wet-warm, the sky low-clouded; the heavy air lies still. A few kilometers across semiurban sprawl and we are at our base, a country hotel of some pretensions set in a recent park. Here too the somnolence of the trough of the afternoon: we disperse to our rooms, send for mineral water, take stock. "Château Haut-Brion 8.45 A.M.," my diary says; we had been bidden to a *dégustation* of the new wines. Now, I've tasted rough, unready claret off the wood; I've drunk mature Haut-Brion; I have never tasted Haut-Brion at Haut-Brion for breakfast.

If daunted, we tell ourselves that this is what we have come for: a round of private visits to some wine châteaux in this very week of the Fête de la Fleur, the flowering of the vine, as pure an enterprise for pleasure as has come my way in many a long year. To the dedicated, the names of the *grands crus classés* are magic. Latour . . . Margaux . . . Mouton . . . We shall be tasting at these, eating and drinking at Lafite, at Chevalier, attend the fête at Ducru-Beaucaillou, sleep at Château Loudenne on the Garonne. . . .

I have not been to Bordeaux for a good many years; too many. Nor ever known it well. Yet in a sense I *was* there. A day is lacking—whatever else it may have contained—if I have not drunk a little wine. For half a century or more I have drunk wine in and of many countries, many soils, climates, vines, seeking what is honestly made, good of its kind; I have been happy for weeks on end on the Italian neighbor's wine of the year, been overwhelmed a few times by the beauty and stature of a burgundy or a hock, yet the lodestar was ever claret—*ci-gît le coeur*—my true love always returned to the Médoc, the Graves, the Pomerol, and the Sauternes.

We are five friends travelling. Three men, two women. Michel Lemonnier is a professional wine writer, French, cherubic, equable. He takes in what he sees and hears, and talks in charming poetic images (shades of Léon-Paul Fargue). Richard Olney, less equable: he is a painter, a passionate oenophile, a very bright light indeed in the international cookery world. He is an American from the Midwest who has spent most of his adult life in France, where he is held in much affection and esteem. He takes his wine and food *au sérieux* (as well he might). It is these two, Richard and Michel, who have the Bordelais entrées, who made it all come true. L., Irish, J., Californian, sustain our party with their good humor, enthusiasm, and charm; they are marvellous observers and are not going to miss a thing. Both have dazzling looks. By and large, we shall be presentable in the eyes of our hosts. (We are all well spoken in French.)

———

HAUT-BRION. We're on the dot. Sky still low and gray, warmth oppressive; a climate more beneficial, perhaps, to vines than men? We are shown around the *chai,* the sheds, the cellars, slowly, talkatively. What strikes is the order, the sacred immaculateness, the quiet. The steel vats gleam; the long, straight lines of barrels look as if they have been waxed; the bungs are glass. The whole has the aesthetic appeal of geometry plus spit and polish raised to an *n*th degree. Madame Y., who must have told it all before, radiates intelligent affection, confidence in what she is doing, what they are all doing—the men and women who work together on a wine estate, the *vignerons,* from owner to *régisseur,* plough hand, cook and bottle washer, are a team, a family, a happy ship.

A cellarman appears, five large tulip glasses dangling from one well-used hand. He taps a barrel; a thin red thread curves into the glass. "Château Haut-Brion 1977." We look, we inhale, we draw in our mouthful: we chew, we *think.* It is a slow process (one is standing, if not always standing still), utterly absorbing and near an ordeal—the raw tannin puckers the inside of the cheeks, rasps the throat like claws, while at the kernel one finds a notion of . . . what? texture, structure, multiplicities of scents, analogous tastes; divines staying power, future harmonies. How? It's a mysterious process, essentially private, individual—who can ever get inside someone else's palate?—*and yet,* there are rules, measures of consensus, codes of communication. We have pretty good instruments nowadays to tell us the amount of alcohol or yeast or sugar present in a wine, and very useful they are, but that live individual testing by human beings is still an essential pointer at every stage of the making, upbringing, and preservation of wine. What makes a credible, an effective wine taster? Attention, memory, and, I would say, a natural gift, an inherited palate, subsequently trained. There must be interest, love; also a willingness to understand nature, and that of course goes for everything from choosing the right soil—at what angle does it take the sun? how is the slope drained?—to the planting and the tending, the fermenting, fining, shipping, till the right true end: the wine at its peak in the bottle, on the table, in the glass in your hand.

Meanwhile, the wine, that 1977, is in its first infancy, kicking infancy (promising too, contrary to much that has been heard). The 1976, next, is already a degree more tamed. The 1975 is not. We spit the wines, of course (L. a bit unsure at first, as we had been pulling her leg, saying it was an art and had to be done from one side of the mouth); even so, the vinous fumes are powerful; one's being yearns for a crust. There *is* no crust. (Tomorrow I shall fill my pockets with our breakfast bread.) Two more *dégustations* ahead this morning before lunch, and we are wondering about staying the course. Only Richard takes it in his unflagging stride. As we emerge, we walk into a violent thunderstorm—black clouds poised dramatically over fairy-tale turrets. We drive into and through Bordeaux with water gushing along the streets hub high. Everybody prays that there may be no hail.

LAFITE. Here the beauty of the *chai* is of a darker and more ancient order. If Haut-Brion has affinity with a royal yacht, Lafite makes one think of a cathedral. No stainless steel here; Lafite still vinifies its wine in those immense, plain wooden vats, and in the cellar a great range of barrels looms in Rembrandtesque penumbra where quiet men—maturing wine needs silence—move about their skilled, deliberate tasks.

Noon. The hour when one no longer tastes but swallows. And what one gets, and needs, is—praise be to this good Bordelais custom—a glass or two of well-chilled champagne. Before, we make the *tour de la propriété*. The storm has cleared the air and sky; we have a flawless blue day freshened by a light wind. The vines bask in the sun, bordered where they end by a row of red roses now in flower (another charming custom). We step inside: Château Lafite is very pretty, a good deal of Louis Seixe, some Second Empire, not too formal or cluttered. From the red salon (and that refreshing ice bucket)—we are being received, most charmingly, by the *régisseur* and his wife, Monsieur et Madame Jean Creté—we pass into the harmonious dining room, eggshell green and white, and settle around an oval table beneath a chandelier, trying to divide our attention not too unevenly between the conversation and the wines. The conversation is good too. Madame Creté has many well-told tales about the Bordelais Orders, the Commanderies, and the great feasts of the viticultural year, the Bans des Vendanges, the Fête de St Vincent, the Fête de la Fleur, upon us tomorrow. With our luncheons we are offered three clarets, Château Duhart-Milon '66, Château Lafite '66, and Lafite '55. How often is one able to drink a 1955? or a Lafite? I am very happy; I am also enchanted and surprised by the elegance and balance of the Duhart-Milon, a (4me) *grand cru classé* and for some time past perhaps not quite a household word. (The vineyard is next, and now also belongs to Lafite.)

DUCRU-BEAUCAILLOU. The château of the lyrical name that makes the lovely wine. It is the day of the fête. Jean-Eugène Borie, the owner, is this year's host. *Vignerons, négociants,* ornate members of the Commanderies du Bontemps de Médoc et des Graves and aspirants to the Commanderie who will be invested on the terrace this morning—all are milling about the grounds. Once again the brilliant sun and the light breeze. Monsieur le Ministre has arrived, and the cheerful charade of citations, the enrobing (and almost instant disrobing—you may not take it with you) of the neophytes, is under way. Aperitif, two white wines, on the lawn, followed by the banquet for four hundred and forty—forty-six tables for ten—under one marquee (hot). Speeches: M. le Ministre and responses, *before* we eat. There is a band. The wines read spectacular—in the drinking, their right true end, they do not give their best. They are warm. *Here* it is the fault only of circumstances; nobody can expect to be able to bring up some five hundred bottles of vintage claret from cellar-cool to tables at the same right moment, but the result remains sad. Blood-warm, the Margaux 1970, a Rausan-Ségla, is in disarray; it bludgeons rather than refreshes; the beauty of the 1967 Haut-Brion is dissipated almost within seconds in the glass. Richard steps in and organizes a limited rescue operation; by the time the cheeses and the last glorious wine, the 1961 Ducru-Beaucaillou, arrive, our table's share has been gently cooled down. Small consolation amid the general waste; yes, waste.

This is the perennial problem. A great wine is created by a conjuncture of nature and the skills of men; it has taken years on years of dedicated labor, anxiety, care, expense—everything has come right; now to what end? Who will drink it in what spirit, what physical conditions? A well-born wine, a well-bred wine, how often, how seldom, will it be well *drunk?* (We can replay the concerto if we have listened perfunctorily or been interrupted by the telephone; the wine will have gone forever.)

ST. YZONE DU MÉDOC. Château Loudenne. We have come up north and will be spending the night at this most ravishing, low-built, rose-washed château. It belongs to the Gilbeys (since 1875) and is now managed

by Martin Bamford, with Priscilla Bonham-Carter looking after the—exquisite—hospitality. (Here we have a
young Englishwoman who knows her wine and shows it,
and the Médocien professionals, a closed-shop, insular
community, accepting her with admiration and respect.)
We have tea on the long terrace in the slanting afternoon
sun, the vines standing close behind us like a rising tide,
beyond them the Garonne, tranquil and wide. Sails pass
slowly.

There is a dinner party for twelve tonight. The
sequence of wines has not been revealed; our hostess,
who has chosen them, is playing a game with us. Before
each plate—*comme il se doit*—there are *large*, thin, *plain*
tulip-shaped glasses, polished to a sparkle. I count four.
Decanters appear in turn and time (that is, before the
food they are to accompany); temperatures are right. First
wine is that very pretty dry white, Château Loudenne '77;
most of us know it. For it appears a great fish on a long
white platter, a bar grilled over twigs of vine. The first red
is a Loudenne '66 in magnums—a lovely big wine (still
cool in the glass, which *is* the way to get the best out of a
fine red; and how often has this been said in print in
Britain and in France, and how little it is heeded by the
wine-drinking and -serving public who yet devour so
much wine literature; how bedrock that pernicious non-
sense about *chambrer*, which, haven't we heard it before?
dates from a time when dining rooms were only just less
freezing than deep cellars). As for the guessing, most of
us (not I) quite soon tumble on the year but make wrong
stabs at various St. Estèphes for the *cru*. By any name the

La Vie de Château

Loudenne was well done by the roast leg of lamb and mound of fresh-picked *haricots verts*. *Le Bordeaux,* as they say, *sur la viande*. On the whole, food in the region plays second fiddle; owners often do not live in their châteaux and so use caterers when they entertain there, or everyone is busy doing something else and the cellarman's or cooper's wife, who may herself be a packer or work the labelling machine, slaps some beefsteaks on the grill. At subtly anglicized Loudenne, the food (fish charred, lamb pink) was simple and superb. On the cheeses we were presented with a Château de Pez 1945. After drinking deep of wine in youthful strength, there is particular pleasure in turning to the more fugitive complexity of an older wine. And the older wine generally gains by this progression. I would never choose to offer anything older than 1962 without leading up to it with a younger brother or cousin. Our '45 was absorbingly discussed. Michel Lemonnier finally got it right. We rounded off with a Sauternes (on strawberries). It had grown very dark in color, so we were hard put to get the year, 1967, which seemed too young for all that amber. Nor did we guess the wine. The nearest we got to it, geographically, that is, was Château Rieussec. It was, in fact, a Château Yquem. Later, much later, we returned to the long drawing room; the French windows were open to the summer night, the vines lay still under a slim moon, and the low ships were gliding across the view. The mood of the party was serene with that surge of optimism of spirit and physical well-being that comes after a very good wine drunk in congenial company at a leisurely pace.

AND WHAT are we up to tomorrow? we would ask when we were saying each other good-night. What are the plans? We're heading south again, says J., who does most of the driving, into the Sauternoise—we are lunching at Château Yquem (as of course we all know). Too good to be true, L. says; we're living in a dream. We are. Of visual beauty, of old trees, graceful architecture, and vineyards trimmed with roses; a dream too of harmonious existence, continuity, of men and women working in accord with their own nature and with nature. (Statistics say that people of the Bordelais live longer and enjoy more freedom from dread disease than elsewhere, and for once the statistics well may be right.) Many do here as their fathers did before them: a life to be born into. For us, it is what L. speaks of as our *arrière-dernière soirée,* the night before the night before the last day but one (it sounds just as Wonderlandish in English). Well; tomorrow Yquem.

Hundreds of wine estates, *crus artisans, crus bourgeois,* striving for quality, for excellence; above them the *grands crus classés,* the aristocracy, as it were; at the apex the almost royal rank of the first growth, the *premiers grands crus,* the illustrious four (now five) of the Médoc/Graves so styled in 1855, plus Château Ausonne, Cheval Blanc, Pétrus, with a handful of others in the St. Emilion and Pomerol. One, only one, *grand premier cru* at Sauternes. There are *premiers crus* there (without the *grand*), wonderful wines made at Climens, Guirraud, Lafaurie-Peyraguey. . . . There too they harvest the berries, not the whole grapes, the berries one by one, selected day after day in the fullness only of their individual ripeness often attained dangerously late in frost-menaced November, but Yquem is both a symbol and a summit. Here, the pursuit of quality is driven to quixotic limits—the harvest may go on into December, every drop of wine is nursed in barrel for three years, and the yield is infinitesimal. In bad years there is none. In good, it is one vine = one glass of Château Yquem. (At Oporto it is one bottle of port per vine, and *that* is regarded as awesomely, bankruptingly low.)

The *chai* is small. It looks, and much of it is, handmade. Here again the symmetry, the shining order, the quiet devoted work . . .

Là tout n'est qu'ordre et beauté . . .

Once more we stroll along a vineyard in the sun, make initial conversation in a drawing room, champagne in hand, assemble around a formally set table. Our hosts are the present owners, a young couple, the Comte and Contesse de Lur Saluces, in whose family Yquem has been since 1785. Now it is delightful to round off a good dinner with a glass of Sauternes; in fact, there is something unfinished about ending on a dry red wine; all the same I am curious and a little quailing at the prospect of drinking a big, sweet white wine through a whole meal, midday at that. We scan the menu in front of us (no need here to pretend the furtive glance): interesting; there will be an equivalent of the sorbet interval, a simple red wine in the middle. We begin with a true Sauternes, a Château de

Fargues 1970 (the vineyard next to Yquem), cold, uncloy-
ing, delicious, marrying rather well with the sole and
crayfish dish. Starting on the roast duck, we help ourselves to a cool young nameless claret *en carafe,* and it
does refresh our palate; quite soon the appearance of the
first of the Château Yquems, a '69, is welcome. Needless
to say that it is sumptuous, notable that it goes entirely
well with the duck and acceptably with the cheeses. Well-
being spreads; conversation flows. I see, but don't really
take in, some dark specks moving about the white damask
cloth. Oh, ants, says the Comtesse; they love our wine,
can't keep them away. A bottle, two bottles of Château
Yquem appear. We sketch an equivalent of saluting. Irrepressible Richard loudly states that the pudding served
with it is too sweet. Otherwise, euphoria. I try to give
myself to the luscious, romantic wine (shall I ever drink
its like again?), yet when in France you must not sit mute.
My host has been asking me if people drink much wine in
my novels. Never stop, I say; I've been scolded about
that. "Yquem?" I haven't dared, I tell him, go further
than Suduiraut. "*C'est un bon vin,*" says the Comte. I
return to the one in my glass, vaguely aware of the small
gray shape, thumb-size, moving on the cloth. DT's?
Michel Lemmonier leaps off his chair and emits a great
shriek, "*MOUSE!*" (He speaks no English.) Nobody else
turns a hair. Oh, yes, says the Comtesse, the '37 . . . they
will come when we open that. . . .

In the car afterwards, we quiz Michel. How did you
know that one word? "*Mickey* . . ." he says. So much for
the language of Milton and Keats.

La Vie de Château

LAST DAY. Léognan. Domaine de Chevalier, where
Claude Ricard makes some of the great wines of the
Grave, red and white, rich, consistent wines. The ambi-
ence of hospitality has its own style on every estate. Here
it is family luncheon, Sunday luncheon. Mme. Ricard asks
if we like oysters; they've just arrived by fast car from the
sea at Arcachon; then packs us off to join her husband,
who is decanting in the *chai.* "*Il travaille pour nous.*"
Straightaway he explains what we are going to drink and
what he is going to do there. There'll be white Domaine
de Chevalier in magnums, then we'll be confronted
simultaneously with three red wines with the main
course: a Latour, a Lafite, a Chevalier. He will not tell us
the year—one pointer: it will be the same for all three, not
a great, great year, a good one. We shall *not* be told which
wine is which. "With these three it ought to be easy?
Don't be too sure! *I* might find it hard to spot my own
wine." For Claude Ricard is going to put himself in the
dark as well. (Yes, that can be managed. Each decanter is
stoppered with the right name-branded cork. Later,
someone else brings the bottles up into the house and
places them on the table in random order; M. Ricard
takes out the corks and distributes them in his trouser
pockets, right decanter in right pocket, middle in back
pocket, left in left.) We are a tight table of fifteen:
Madame's mother, a young child, adolescent children,
grown-up children, a son and daughter-in-law, handsome, animated faces, lively interest in what is going to
happen. Introductions, criss-crossing of handshakes.

Richard and Michel flank Madame, who explains that they play the wine game in some form every Sunday. Her husband is very much the conjuror and taskmaster. How neatly he pours two fingers of wine into each glass, a touch less for the very young. (Oh, the uncouth, spoil-all slopping to the brim! Then no wine can breathe or give out or develop—will some of us never learn?) He asks us to begin slowly. Not a sip before we've swirled and sniffed and talked about and swirled and sniffed again. (The children are broken to it, but I have to stop L. from a rash swig by a look; she's too far from me for a kick.) We're at once up against an interesting dilemma: the wines are said to be of the same year, but the one in the left glass, to go by look and bouquet, must be older than the other two. We discuss this. . . . What emanates from the right-hand glass is so glorious and deep, surely the Latour? Middle glass is rather closed and discreet. Minutes later this is reversed: middle glass has become opulent, right attenuated. Presently we sip. Permutations continue. . . . I wouldn't have believed it, at a point no one, including its maker, can tell whether the Chevalier is the Latour or not. (When, in its good time, the true Latour does reveal itself, *it does so*.) Great wine in the glass goes once more through a life cycle, its last one, a dumb beginning often, gradual opening to full inherent maturity, softening, thinning, fading. . . . Meanwhile, we have begun to drink more deeply, and to eat, sizzling grilled steaks and mushrooms; using one's mind concurrently does not detract from sensual pleasure; we are still trying to pin down immediate experience in words. It's a good game, a friendly game (as it was at Loudenne), a game for learning, not to score or win—nobody minds a scrap if he or she is wrong—but for learning about the nature of wine, learning to store pleasure. When we break off at an advanced hour of the afternoon I know that there, at the table of this delightful family sharing sensual, civilized pleasure, some wine had found its right, true end.

VENICE IN WINTER

1967

WINTER IN VENICE. Arrival. The moment of doubt: Will it be there, will it have subsisted, this grandest, this strangest, most fabulous of white elephants of the past? Can that magic still work on the inhabitant of an increasingly different world? The handing into the *motoscafo*, the bestowal of luggage—*signori!*—moments of Italian action that can be fraught with strife or pass with luxurious smoothness: the gliding away, ensconced in soft rugs, only the face stung by cold and air; the moment of transition: the curve in the waterway: seeing. Façades, reflections, bridges, perspectives, animation—the great backcloth and the swarming movement: a hundred watercraft cavorting in front of palazzi on palazzi, water-gnawed, extravagant, melancholy, voluptuous, glowing in decay. Here it is, then, laid bare as it were, bare of the dazzle, the panache, the golden banners of high summer, bare to the bone, the perennial, the mysterious beauty of Venice.

After the sleigh ride, after the overwhelming: refuge. Inside a polished walnut, the elegant small hotel. Warmth. Welcome. The major luxuries of travel are a sense of security, freedom from friction—order, comfort, calm. The Italians, in the right mood, when not swung into an opposite direction, have a genius for providing them.

Ten minutes later the urge to set out again, the longing for more. On foot now. This is the city where locomotion itself is pleasure, is ease—a choice between gliding and strolling. Nothing is far because an essence is always here, before one, wherever one happens to be, and round the corner as well. One has only got to look up; to look.

These walks! Round the corner and the next one, and the next. Here there is no wasteland, no dull stretches, no intrusions, no ugliness: the bank is as splendidly housed as the bake shop. And the variety is unending. One can walk for hours, seemingly lost, never quite lost, and not cease to come upon the undiscovered, the rediscovered, the new—come from the sumptuous shop-lined street into a dramatic square, plunge under an archway, follow the boy with the trolley of tangerines, emerge into a triangular *piazetta,* cross the bridge, pass the colonnaded church, over the next bridge, up more steps, through a long street where cabinetmakers are chipping at their trade, take the sharp turning, find sunlight, a market, an asymmetrical piazza, blown by winds, a vast looming church, take another bridge and a street of bright, prosperous food shops, dive into a passage, shoulders touching walls, come out onto a minute widening by a canal.

One stands alone. The water lap-laps against the sides of a small, pink-washed palazzo. The barley-sugar columns framing the windows are exquisite; washing is hanging out. There is one tree.

The very street signs lure one on. Fondamento, Campo, Largo, Riva, Piscina, Calle, Calleone, dedicated to deity, to saints and ages, heraldic animals, and past sensational events. Who can forbear to enter the Sottoportico del' Uccelletto, to follow the Riva degli Due Assassini, the Street of the Almonds, the Narrow Street of the Young Bears?

Seemingly lost; never quite lost. There is the occasional arrow pointing a direction—San Marco. Rialto. Ferrovia. There are, always obliging, never themselves at a loss, the Venetians. The question is simply framed; one names a landmark: Accademia? Piazza? Albergo? "Cross the bridge!" they cry, "*Fa il punte!*" They pronounce *ponte* thus. There follows some eloquent and effective gesture. Another passerby stops in his tracks and takes it up: he is headed, he signs, precisely in that direction; he beckons, ambles on, you follow his swift progress with his burden, a tall pair of gilt candlesticks, a tray of sweetmeats, a string of *fiaschi*, for the Venetians are forever trundling food and drink and chattels from one point of their maze to another. Upon their heads in huge flat baskets or boat-shaped wooden bowls, or propelled on those special trolleys mounted on low wheels and stilts that are able to negotiate steps. "*Gambe!*" they shout, "Mind your legs!" as they come charging down an alleyway five feet wide with their cargo of ship irons or wine. Recently some of the younger porters have changed their warning cry to a simple-minded "Hello!"

Winter belongs to the Venetians; the inhabitants of the large and teeming city have come back into their own. The air is filled with the ring of their voices, with those curious local cadences, both harsh and lilting, singing out greetings and good wishes. For it is the long, slow, festive season that stretches though practically the whole of December on to Twelfth Night, and the teeming city, one now realizes, is really a small town—*Dottore, buon giorno—Buon giorno, Padre—Serafina, ciao—Tante cose—Auguri, auguri. . . .*

At every turning women stop to meet; men raise their hats to one another. There are few visible tourists, no hordes milling in Piazza San Marco; this does not mean that the streets are empty at all hours; the rhythm of native Venetian life is as regular as the tides. At noon and again at sunset people pour en masse into streets and squares to stand and talk, drink coffee, eat cakes and ices before drifting home or into the *trattorie* for more solid meals; low tide comes by eleven at night and during the long, postprandial hours of the afternoon, when all at once there will be space and a great stillness—it is now that the magic is at its most potent and one can hear the sounds of water, the small sounds the gondolas make straining at their moorings, and the sound of footfall upon the slender bridge.

It is the spectators' city, the place of ecstatic wanderings; it is also the place of perpetual covetousness. One covets what one sees—the silks, the leather, the ornaments, the hundred handsome things made by hand, displayed with such love and art. The seductiveness of those shop windows, the intimacy. And the food: surely nowhere else in the world is food made to look as beautiful as it does in Venice. There is the color and extravagant variety of all that sea life that comes out of the Adriatic; there is the dewy, newborn freshness of the roots and leaves grown on the mainland, the Veneto di Terra Fiona; there are the simple, the biblical shapes of bread and cheeses—the very colors and shapes of the fruit and loaves and fishes that have been used for centuries by Venetian artists, by Carpaccio, Bellini, Tintoretto, Veronese, in their allegories and painted feasts.

To see it in its subtle glory one must see the food of Venice as it arrives at daybreak at the quays of the Rialto markets, the *pescheria* and the *erberia,* and watch the cargo-gondolas being unloaded in that first blue and hazy Adriatic light. One will never forget that sudden transcendent quality of ordinary things, the glow of the fruit in its own leaves, the purple and green of artichokes with bushy tails, the delicacy of the sea creatures, silver, lilac— pale and coral red.

From the barges to the vendors' stalls. Vegetables are built into banks, fish laid out in patterns on marble slabs, and with what skill and care, what instinctive taste—that pyramid over there of saffron and scarlet peppers, that spray of spinach assembled leaf by curly leaf, that sea spider flanked by rosy prawns and scrolls of sole—with what patience, what devotion! In the cold, the stone cold of this December dawn, bare hands are plunged ungrudgingly again and again into the dripping baskets to create these ephemeral still lifes. And for whose eyes? The shopkeepers' and the greengrocers' and the restaurant keepers' who come morning after morning to buy their day's supply—surely we have here one of the purest examples of art for art's sake? Perhaps there is in the people of Venice still something of the human spirit that conceived of the tour de force of building a city in the sea and then, far from contenting itself with a primitive dwelling or a Spartan fortress, went on to create a place of incomparable fantasy and splendor.

A splendor that has endured, as have its people. For how many centuries more? How many ocean tides, how many winters? Let us go there while we may.

CHRONOLOGY

⁓

"The Anchor and the Balloon," *Encounter*, August 1954.

"Notes on a Journey in Portugal," *Vogue*, 15 January 1959.

"The Quality of Travel," *Esquire*, November 1961.

"Portrait Sketch of a Country," *Esquire*, December 1964.

"A Journey in Yugoslavia," *Venture*, April/May 1966.

"Venice in Winter," *Venture*, November 1968.

"La Vie de Château," *Harpers & Queen*, May 1979.

"A Homecoming," *The Spectator*, 6 October 2001.

ABOUT THE AUTHOR

SYBILLE BEDFORD was born in Charlottenburg, Germany, in 1911 and was privately educated in Italy, England, and France. She published her first book, *The Sudden View: A Mexican Journey*, in 1953. By the time it was reissued, seven years later, as *A Visit to Don Otavio*, it had won a reputation as a classic of travel writing. *A Legacy* appeared in 1956, and three other novels followed: *A Favourite of the Gods* (1963), *A Compass Error* (1968), and *Jigsaw* (1989), which was shortlisted for the Booker Prize.

The Best We Can Do (1958), an account of the murder trial of Dr. John Bodkin Adams, was the first of Mrs. Bedford's writings on law at work. She has reported on some of the most important criminal trials of our times, including those of Jack Ruby and the former staff at Auschwitz. *The Faces of Justice* (1961) collected her observations on the courts in England, Germany, Austria, Switzerland, and France. *As It Was* (1990) brought together further essays in justice as well as her celebrated writings on food, wine, and European travel.

In 1973 Mrs. Bedford published a two-volume authorized life of her friend and mentor Aldous Huxley. Stephen

Spender called this book "one of the masterpieces of biography."

Mrs. Bedford lives in London, where she is a vice president of English PEN. In 1981 she was made an officer of the Order of the British Empire and in 1994 was elected a Companion of Literature by the Royal Society of Literature.